ROCK SOLID
TRUST

TRUSTING GOD WHEN LIFE IS HARD

VIRGINIA GROUNDS

WESTBOW
PRESS®
A DIVISION OF THOMAS NELSON
& ZONDERVAN

Copyright © 2018 Virginia Grounds.

Edited by Mary Park

All rights reserved. No part of this book may be used or reproduced by any means, graphic, electronic, or mechanical, including photocopying, recording, taping or by any information storage retrieval system without the written permission of the author except in the case of brief quotations embodied in critical articles and reviews.

WestBow Press books may be ordered through booksellers or by contacting:

WestBow Press
A Division of Thomas Nelson & Zondervan
1663 Liberty Drive
Bloomington, IN 47403
www.westbowpress.com
1 (866) 928-1240

Because of the dynamic nature of the Internet, any web addresses or links contained in this book may have changed since publication and may no longer be valid. The views expressed in this work are solely those of the author and do not necessarily reflect the views of the publisher, and the publisher hereby disclaims any responsibility for them.

This book is a work of non-fiction. Unless otherwise noted, the author and the publisher make no explicit guarantees as to the accuracy of the information contained in this book and in some cases, names of people and places have been altered to protect their privacy.

Any people depicted in stock imagery provided by Getty Images are models, and such images are being used for illustrative purposes only. Certain stock imagery © Getty Images.

ISBN: 978-1-9736-2752-4 (sc)
ISBN: 978-1-9736-2751-7 (hc)
ISBN: 978-1-9736-2753-1 (e)

Library of Congress Control Number: 2018905434

Print information available on the last page.

WestBow Press rev. date: 5/24/2018

Scripture quotations marked (NIV) are taken from the Holy Bible, New International Version®, NIV®. Copyright © 1973, 1978, 1984, 2011 by Biblica, Inc.™ Used by permission of Zondervan. All rights reserved worldwide. www.zondervan.com The "NIV" and "New International Version" are trademarks registered in the United States Patent and Trademark Office by Biblica, Inc.

Scripture quotations are from the ESV® Bible (The Holy Bible, English Standard Version®), copyright © 2001 by Crossway, a publishing ministry of Good News Publishers. Used by permission. All rights reserved.

Scripture quotations marked HCSB®, are taken from the Holman Christian Standard Bible®, Copyright © 1999, 2000, 2002, 2003, 2009 by Holman Bible Publishers. Used by permission. HCSB® is a federally registered trademark of Holman Bible Publishers.

Scripture quotations taken from the New American Standard Bible® (NASB), Copyright © 1960, 1962, 1963, 1968, 1971, 1972, 1973, 1975, 1977, 1995 by The Lockman Foundation Used by permission. www.Lockman.org

Scripture taken from the New King James Version®. Copyright © 1982 by Thomas Nelson. Used by permission. All rights reserved.

Scripture taken from the King James Version of the Bible.

CONTENTS

Dedication xi
Acknowledgements xiii
Foreword xv
Introduction xix

Chapter 1   The Rock of Trust 1
Chapter 2   Trusting God with Imperfection 8
Chapter 3   What's The Difference in a Word? 19
Chapter 4   Trusting When Betrayed 26
Chapter 5   Trusting When Exhausted 36
Chapter 6   Trust Even When Threatened 46
Chapter 7   Trusting Where God Leads 60
Chapter 8   Trust When Suffering 71
Chapter 9   Cornerstone of Trust 79
Chapter 10   Trusting the Process Patiently 88
Chapter 11   Tools for Rock Solid Trust 97
Chapter 12   Desired Result 103
Chapter 13   My Trust Building Journey of Faith .. 108

How Do I Become a Christian? 115
References 119

My soul finds rest in God alone;
My salvation comes from him.
He alone is my rock and my salvation;
He is my fortress, I will never be shaken.
Psalm 62:1-2

DEDICATION

This book is dedicated to the One who gives me reason to trust – and that is Jesus. It is also dedicated to my husband, Gene, who encourages me in everything God gives me to complete. His patient understanding and encouragement have inspired me beyond my abilities. And to my grandsons as they embark on manhood, may you have a Rock Solid Trust in Jesus to help you through any hardships life throws your way.

ACKNOWLEDGEMENTS

The support and encouragement of friends and family has been very humbling. I am thankful for each one who took part in making this book possible. To Mary Park for the hours of editing you contributed, I thank you. You have been such an inspiration to me, and my admiration for you has grown even more through this process. To Kaye Johns, my ministry advisor and mentor, I thank you for your wisdom and encouragement through the years. You have kept me pressing on.

And I am so appreciative of those who read chapters and gave amazing encouragement through their comments: Mary Park, Kaye Johns, Kay Daigle, Pastor Jim Pasley, Susan Butler, Gene Grounds, Debbie Stuart, Terri Burnett, Janie Odell, Kim Shirley, and Lisa Clark. God has used each of you to affirm this work through your prayers and encouragement.

Majestic Inspirations Ministry and the publishing of this book would not have been possible without the additional support of Teri Quance, Bob and Della Best, Diane Clark, Mickey and Mary Ann Foret, Tim and Rhonda Parker, Don and Lena Gibson, Jim and Janice Pitts, John and Deanna Keirnan, Tom and Karen Singleterry, Veronica Sites and many others – you know who you are. Thank you for allowing God to use you to help others grow in their faith and trust of our Savior Jesus.

FOREWORD

Learning to trust God when life is hard is the focus of *Rock Solid Trust*. You'll find real life stories of people in the Bible filled with action and emotion that we can easily relate to. The stories reveal the impact of broken trust in those lives and show clearly how God worked in every circumstance. Each story affirms the importance of trusting Him and building our confidence to face difficult times today.

Through current day stories and personal testimony, the author reveals how active and present God is for those who trust Him. You will find her insights inspiring and trust-building for those seeking to grow their faith. Bible Study questions at the end of each chapter provide direction for deeper study.

How vital it is today in the upheaval we see in the world around us, that we trust in God's power, presence and sovereignty.

Kaye Johns
Co-Founder
PrayerPower Ministries

Rock Solid Trust
Trust in the LORD forever, for the LORD,
the LORD Himself is the Rock eternal.
Isaiah 26:4

INTRODUCTION

Recently I looked at a project I was working on and thought, *what were you thinking?* Feeling insecure about my ability to do the project, fear took hold. The next morning as I was reading my Bible Study, a statement seemed magnified just for me. It said, "What God has put before you, He will equip you to accomplish for His purpose."

Insecurity is something a lot of people deal with at some point in life. The root of insecurity is fear of the future, uncertainty and lack of confidence causing distrust that anything can be different than it is now. Fear weakens our ability to trust others, and especially weakens our faith and trust in God. And, it weakens our confidence in doing what God has given us to complete. But God will always enable us when He gives us a project that will glorify Him and serve His purpose.

As I have taught and listened to the stories of others about living in this ever-changing society, a common thread has emerged. That is a lack of trust, or shattered trust, from circumstances beyond personal control. Why? As the old saying goes, "the times, they are a-changing." We are seeing more violence on the news every day. We are hearing things that were once unmentionable, but are now put on the screen for all to see, and for our children to ask questions. Time after time, we hear of people who have proven to be untrustworthy due to betrayal, abuse, deception and so much more.

Perhaps your trust has faltered because of a situation in one of those areas. If so, there is good news for you. There is One who does not change, who is faithful and trustworthy. He is the One that is rock solid. You can trust God for the future. He already has a plan for you.

This book is written for the purpose of directing your attention to the reasons why you can trust Him. It is written to help you understand that when everything around you is crumbling, when trust is shattered and doubts enter your mind, The Rock of our salvation will never shatter. He will never crumble under the weight of your burdens and your doubts. He is strong enough to carry you through whatever is troubling to you. He can, and He will, carry you as you place your trust in Him.

In traveling to Haiti and El Salvador on missions in the past, I saw on the faces of women the helplessness that comes from their mistreatment. I saw on the faces of men the hopelessness of poverty. But I also saw the hope they have in God because their trust in Him is solid. If these people from around the world who have suffered so much can trust God, then surely we can build a stronger faith and trust in Him ourselves.

Let's commit to seeking Him in a new and fresh way as we look at the lives of Moses, David, Jehoshaphat and Paul, great men of the Bible who trusted God when others did not, who trusted when exhausted from fighting the same old battles and when overwhelmed by circumstances. And let's commit to learn from the words and works of Jesus for life today.

So, how do you build a deeper trust in God, a trust that does not falter, no matter what happens?

- By *planting* the seeds of truth from His word deep into your heart and mind.
- By *looking* at who God is in scripture.

- By *looking* at how His character and identity apply to your own life.
- By *praying* His word back to Him in praise and thanksgiving.

You will find questions related to the above statements at the end of each chapter to help you strengthen your trust in God. I encourage you to work through the questions and pray regarding your responses to the **Trust Building Actions** and **Questions for Personal Growth.**

Throughout the book, as you look at the scriptures, I encourage you to read them in four different ways for personal growth. It is a method of studying the Bible using the acrostic **R.E.A.D**. That is, **read, example, application and direction**. This method of study is similar to one I learned from the Minister to Women at my church at the time, Debbie Stuart, in her book *20 Minutes a Day for the Rest of Your Life*.[1] Debbie got the idea for an acrostic guide to study from attending an Anne Graham Lotz Bible Study Workshop a few years ago. And I loved that approach to scripture so developed another like it. I have learned that if you use a system for personal study, you retain what you learn better and longer. Find one that works for you and stick to it. If you will think in terms of four things as you study, I believe this method will enhance your insight and understanding.

And so, I want to stop here for a moment and explain it. We will use Deuteronomy 32:4 as an example of how to study using the acrostic R.E.A.D .

> The Rock – His work is perfect; all His ways are entirely just. A faithful God, without prejudice, He is righteous and true.
> Deuteronomy 32:4 HCSB

R – Read

First, *read the verse*. The scriptures are the truths of God's Word: God is THE ROCK, His work is perfect, His ways are just, and He is faithful, righteous and true. Those words are true. Read as a student with Jesus as your teacher.

E – Example

Second, *what is the example?* An example is a characteristic of, or illustration of, a general rule. It is something to be illustrated or exemplified; a person or thing regarded in terms of their fitness to be imitated. Who or what is the illustration used to teach something God wants you to know about Himself, or something, from a particular verse or section of scripture. What is the focus of the verse?

What example did Moses use in teaching his audience? The example is the Rock to identify God as strong, immovable and always the same. He is the focus. The lesson for his audience is *the identity of God in this passage as the one and only God (The Rock) and a description of His character.*

A – Application

Next, make an application. *The Application* is for you, the reader, to ask the question, how does this apply to me personally? *God the rock is strong; I can lean on Him. He will treat me fairly, always doing what is just for me. Because He is faithful, I can trust Him with my life and needs. He is righteous; there is no wrong in Him so I can know that whatever He does in my life is for my best. And through Him, I can stand rock solid in my faith.*

D – Direction

Read the scripture, look for the example given, ask how it

applies to your life, and then, *determine the direction* God is leading you as a result. Direction is a course along which someone or something moves; the course that must be taken in order to reach a destination. Direction is the general aim or purpose in following the guidance of someone. It is an authoritative order or command.

Therefore, what course of action do you need to apply or change in your direction in order to fulfill God's purpose for you? This involves prayer. This is where you pray according to the scripture and application for you. Possibly something like this:

God my Rock, thank you for who you are in my life. Thank you for showing me that I can trust you, confident that you always know what is best for me. Help me to accept your wisdom and purpose in my life. I am committing anew to you to stand strong and firm in my faith, trusting in you to provide the direction needed for serving your purpose. Amen!

That is a prayer example showing how you can pray straight from scripture by applying R.E.A.D to your study time and using what you learn for God's glory and your benefit.

My prayer for you is that God will use this book to remove any doubts you may have about trusting Him and to fill your heart with a song of praise as you trust Him in every situation. You can trust in the love of God because He is bigger and stronger and more than you can ever imagine, and yet, He loves you. You can trust that!

Serving Him,
–Virginia–

Trusting God's Love

Higher than the heavens
Deeper than the sea
Wider than the earth is round
That's your love for me.
More than any person
More than earthly wealth
More than silver or gold,
Precious jewels or anything else
That's how much you love me
That's how much you care
That's a love I cannot explain
Yet, of which, I am very aware.
So thank You LORD for loving me
Even knowing mistakes I've made
Thank you for grace and forgiveness
And the life-changing sacrifice you gave.
Your love is amazing
It's so high and deep and wide.
How can I not but trust you
Knowing you are always by my side.

–Virginia–

CHAPTER 1

The Rock of Trust

> Trust in the Lord with all your heart and lean
> not on your own understanding;
> in all your ways acknowledge Him and
> He will make your paths straight.
> Proverbs 3:5–6

What does trust mean to you? Does it come easily, or do you have a difficult time trusting? Without trust, it is difficult to move forward in life with confidence that your needs will be met. The meaning of the word *trust* is "to lean on, rely upon, to have confidence in." Without trust, you may lean and find yourself falling with nothing, or no one, to hold you up. You may rely on people who are untrustworthy or place your confidence in things that do not satisfy, and then you wonder why you feel so discontent and insecure.

> *"Without trust, you may lean and find yourself falling with nothing, or no one, to hold you up"*

A life lived without trusting in God is an empty life without hope for the future. It is a life without the only source of strength that can walk with you through the valleys of life to the goodness beyond.

And so, do you have a lack of confidence? If so, the root may be fear that stems from a lack of trust. Please begin this book with prayer, asking God to show and teach you how to be confident by learning to trust Him more.

If you read all of Deuteronomy 32, you will find God's message to the people through His servant Moses. You will find in this chapter words of action at the very beginning in verses 1–2. These words of action are, "Pay attention, heavens, and I will speak; listen, earth, to the words of my mouth."

"Pay attention, heavens"—that is the abode of God and the place where angels dwell. He then said, "Listen, earth, to the words of my mouth." Because God is the Lord of *all* the heavens and earth, Moses began his message by reminding the people of the sovereignty of God in all of creation. He gave a command and an action plan in one word: *listen*.

How many times have you sat in church and watched as someone nodded off in sleep as the pastor was preaching the Word of God. Moses was saying to this group of people, "Don't nod off while I am speaking. You need to hear every word I am saying." Probably all of us could take a lesson from this strong command. Listen when God speaks through those He has chosen to speak His Word. You never know when the message may be just exactly what you needed to hear at the time.

While we were sitting in church one morning, our pastor spoke about things that addressed many family situations we were facing. It was a powerful, motivating, spiritually rich message. But at the beginning of the message, I noticed my husband was distracted and nodding off. So I did what any good wife would do—I nudged him. God had a message for both of us that He didn't want us to miss. He said through Moses, and He says to us today, "Listen to the words of my mouth."

You will see in verse 2, Moses began to ask that his teaching would fall upon the people in four different ways:

1. *Fall like rain.* Refreshing and feeding, life-sustaining water. Giving moisture to that which is dry.
2. *Settle like dew.* Dew is only visible when the conditions are right. Make the conditions right in the hearts of your people so Your Word will descend and settle within them.
3. *Fall like gentle rain on new grass.* What do showers on new grass do? They stimulate growth.
4. *Fall like showers on tender plants.* Stimulate growth and provide nutrition needed to see them through the dry times.

Isn't that what we are after as we study the Bible, God's Holy Word? We want to grow in our wisdom and knowledge of Him. Look at God's promise in the book of Hosea:

> Let us strive to know the Lord. His appearance is as sure as the dawn. He will come to us like the rain, like the spring showers that water the land.
> Hosea 6:3 HCSB

We have a promise from God that if we strive to know Him better, His presence in our lives will be a sure thing. And by His presence, He will teach us in a way that we flourish and grow. We have His promise that He will stimulate growth in us as we open our hearts and minds, allowing Him to make conditions right for learning.

Many years ago, I went with friends to a retreat in Colorado that was held on a ranch. The theme was loving Jesus. On the last day, the speaker challenged us to take our Bibles outside, find a place of solitude, and listen for the Lord to speak through His Word. Being a girly girl back then, I didn't want to get my hair messed up or my clothes dirty, so I looked and looked for just the right spot. Finally I saw a slab of concrete and prepared to sit down and open my Bible. But just about the time I was settled, it began to rain. Oh my goodness, you can't believe the grumbling and complaining coming out of my mouth—and God heard every word.

As I gathered my things to go back inside, the Lord spoke through a still small voice as if He were standing right there in front of me. *Virginia, don't you love me enough to sit with me in the rain for a moment?* Whew! My knees gave way and I immediately sat again, knowing I had heard a word from the Lord. The funny thing is that as soon as I opened my Bible again, the rain stopped! But funnier still is that the passage I opened to was Hosea 6:3. As I look back on that occasion, I realize God was testing my love and obedience to Him. He wanted me to recognize that my priorities were messed up—that I was more concerned about my appearance, my hair, and my clothes than I was about spending time in solitude with Him.

God wanted to stimulate spiritual growth and maturity in me. Even though it has been at least twenty years since then, I remember it as if it were yesterday. God wants us to love Him enough to sit with Him in the rain if that's what it takes to get our attention. Why? So we can listen, learn, and grow. God got my attention that day.

In James 4:8, it tells us that when we draw near to God, He will draw near to us. That is what He did for me in that moment, and that is what He will do for you. If you hear what God teaches through His Word, if you come to Him and acknowledge who He is in your life, then there is a trust-building truth that will give you assurance:

- The more we listen, the more we grow.
- The more we grow, the closer we are to God.
- The closer we are to God, the stronger our trust in Him.

Studying the Bible is about new life. It is about growth and relationship. If you want to be able to trust God more, to experience His strength, and to have greater confidence, then you need to read

His Word. You need to listen and ask how it applies to you. Pay attention to what it says and then act upon it.

Trust-Building Action

Based on what you have read in this first chapter, what action do you need to take in order to build your trust?

Read Hebrews 10:22 (NAS): "Let us draw near with a sincere heart in full assurance of faith, having our hearts sprinkled clean from an evil conscience and our bodies washed in pure water."

In this verse, the Bible has four conditions for drawing near to God.

1. *Come to Him with a sincere heart.* When I went before Him that day at the ranch, my heart was not sincere. I was more concerned about the external than I was the internal of my life.
2. *Draw near with full assurance of faith,* knowing He is who He says He is and will do what He says He will do. Have faith, believing in Him for salvation and eternal life.
3. *Come with hearts sprinkled and cleansed from sin.* That took place when Jesus hung on the cross at Calvary and took our sin upon Himself, forgiving sins once and for all. But this also means that as we come to Him, we need to confess the sins of our hearts, minds, and bodies in the here and now. A great verse to pray back to God is: "Wash me thoroughly from my iniquity, and cleanse me from my sin" (Psalm 51:2 ESV).
4. *Bodies washed in pure water.* The only pure water is the Living Water that is Christ Jesus.

And so to fully trust God, you must have faith. You must draw near to God in prayer and ask Him to reveal any weak areas in your ability to trust Him so you will be aware of what action to take.

Then you will be building a greater confidence in your life in order to dispel feelings of insecurity.

Questions for Personal Growth

- How is God revealed through what you have read?

- What character trait of God have you seen that strengthens your trust?

- What seed of truth from His Word will you plant in your heart and mind from this chapter?

And so, in review, you have learned:

- How to study scripture using the READ method of study (see introduction)
- How to grow in trust—listen, read, ask
- How to approach God (Hebrews 10:22 NAS)

    o With a *sincere* heart
    o Full *assurance* of faith
    o *Cleansed* from sin
    o *Washed* in pure water, the Living Water of Christ

CHAPTER 1

R.E.A.D. for Optional Study

Using the READ method of study, write your observations of the verse, example, application, and direction for you from the scripture below.

> Trust in the Lord with all your heart and lean
> not on your own understanding;
> in all your ways acknowledge Him and
> He will make your path straight.
> Proverbs 3:5–6

R

E

A

D

CHAPTER 2

Trusting God with Imperfection

*He is The Rock – His works are perfect; and all His ways are just.
A faithful God who does no wrong, upright and just is He.
Deuteronomy 32:4*

Are you perfect? There was a woman who took perfectionism to the extreme. Her life revolved around keeping the perfect house, cooking the perfect meals and having the perfect family. Her struggle to maintain everything to perfection was costly. Her family suffered because they could not live up to her expectations. She was under constant pressure due to her need to be something not intended. Does anything about this sound familiar to you?

The positive thing about wanting to be perfect is that it means you care. But there is a problem. We are all human. We are not without flaws. We are not perfect no matter how hard we try. Oh, we want to produce the WOW effect, but I believe we need to think about what that says about our focus. Are we focused on what we can do, or on what God can do?

In continuing to read Moses song, there are things to learn about perfection. "I will proclaim the name of the LORD." (Deuteronomy 32:3)

Why is he proclaiming the name of the LORD? *(Proclaim means to announce publicly and officially)*. Moses was not ashamed or embarrassed to speak of God publicly. He was not afraid of offending anyone. In fact, he continued by saying, "Oh, praise the greatness of our God!" Then in verse 4 he said, "He is The Rock – His works are perfect; and all His ways are just. A faithful God who does no wrong, upright and just is He." By using the preposition THE before the name Rock, Moses was pointing out that God is the One and Only God. He is not *a* rock, one among many; He is *The* Rock. There is no other before Him. And so, by identifying God as The Rock, the lesson for us personally is that He is the only One strong enough to catch us when we stumble. Therefore, we can lean on Him without fear of falling. We can trust Him to hold us up when the world around us is crumbling.

Moses began to identify some attributes of God *The* Rock in verse 4. He declared that the works of God are perfect. God the Rock – His *works* are perfect. Now *that* is a big WOW! God's works are perfect!

The word *perfect* from Deuteronomy 32:4 in the original Hebrew is "Tamlym. (ta-meem). From this verse in the Old Testament, the meaning is *the divine standard which man must attain in accordance with the law*. It is important that you remember this definition of the word Tamlyn in the Old Testament as you read further.

In addition, the word perfect means *integrity, entire, complete, without blemish, sincere, undefiled and upright in conduct. What is complete or entirely in accord with truth and fact.*

God created His works perfect, including the first man. But sin entered into mankind through Adam. Therefore, we are not born perfect, but born into sin. We are born with a human nature. And so, if we do not enter into the perfection that is only found in Jesus, our lives are spent striving for perfection we will never achieve apart from Christ. Even then, perfection for us is not complete until we reach our heavenly home.

I know, I know. You may be saying 'but wait a minute; babies are perfect.' Believe me, I can relate. At the time of this writing, I had just spent a week babysitting a new baby in our family. He has the sweetest disposition. He is adorable, and to me – perfect! But as with all babies, they grow to be children, teens and then adults. No one has to teach these toddlers to say no or to hold onto their toys saying "mine." That is because of the sin nature of mankind that all are born into. But we do try to be perfect, don't we?

Are you a perfectionist? Are you a person who wants everything as you want it and feel you are the only one who can make it that way? I know what I am talking about because I used to be that person. A perfectionist is never satisfied with the end result and keeps trying to make it, whatever *it* is, better until they are dragged kicking and screaming from the *it* they are trying to perfect. We look for the perfect relationship, children, job, school, haircut, clothing and homes; but in reality, none of those things are truly perfect. To trust them to satisfy us long-term is to set ourselves up for disappointment.

- Relationships require the work of giving as well as receiving
- Children grow and develop their own personalities
- Jobs change
- Schools have rules
- Hair grows out
- Clothes wear out.
- Homes get old

Nothing we thought was perfect when it was new ever remains the same. Things change, people change, *and we* change.

I learned the hard way that true perfection will never be achieved on this earth. I learned that life is so much easier when I am more flexible and accepting of what *is* rather than what *is not*. I learned that trusting my ability to achieve perfection for myself or something made with my hands was an indication that I was not trusting God in the area of life I was trying to perfect.

Does any of this strike a chord with you? Can you identify with what I am saying? It is only as we trust God with our relationships, children, jobs, homes and daily needs that we will have peace in those areas of our lives. You may have someone close to you that you don't fully trust, but you can trust God *with* that person, releasing him or her into God's care. You can't change the person, but God can.

Read what verses in Hebrews 7 say about perfection, the law and the new covenant.

> If then, perfection came through the Levitical priesthood (for under it the people received the law), what further need was there for another priest to appear.
>
> So the previous command is annulled because it was weak and unprofitable (for the law perfected nothing), but a better hope is introduced, through which we draw near to God. None of this happened without an oath. For others became priests without an oath, but He became a priest with an oath made by the One who said to Him: *The Lord has sworn, and He will not change His mind, you are a priest forever.* So Jesus has also become the guarantee of a better covenant.
> Hebrews 7:11a, 18-22 HCSB

Remember, part of the definition of perfect is *the divine standard by which man must attain according to the Law.* But, as time went by, striving to reach that standard of perfection could not be achieved only by the Law. The Law could not make man perfect, therefore, a new and better covenant was needed and provided.

In Hebrews 7:22 we find that *Jesus is the mediator of a new covenant.* In fact, He has become for you and me the *guarantee* of a covenant that is better than that of the Levitical Priesthood where animals were sacrificed in the days of the Old Testament.

The Bible tells us that without the shedding of blood, there is no remission of sin. The people of the Old Testament days had to go to the temple once a year for the atonement of their sins, but the priests went daily. However, this system was not permanent. It had to be repeated over and over. So God sent His Only Begotten Son, the Lamb of God, to sacrifice Himself once for all people, for all time. That is His gift to us, the gift of Grace in that while we were still sinners, Christ died for us. (Romans 5:8)

When we commit our lives to Christ, we are making covenant with God for living by His divine standard made possible *through* Christ. It was impossible to live by that standard according to the law. A covenant is a binding agreement. God makes covenant with you through Jesus Christ that you will spend eternity with Him, and you make covenant with God through Christ to live by His Word and will for your life.

Therefore, the perfection we are to pursue is spiritual perfection. According to A. W. Tozer, the path to perfection is understanding God's Word and obeying it.

"The word of God well understood and religiously obeyed is the shortest route to spiritual perfection." – A. W. Tozer –[2]

> *"The word of God well understood and religiously obeyed is the shortest route to spiritual perfection."*

Through your commitment to Jesus Christ, God has begun a work of perfection in you. When will perfection be complete? Read Philippians 1:6 to find out. "Being confident of this, that He who started a good work in you will carry it on to completion until the day of Christ Jesus."

When is the day of Christ Jesus? It is the day that Jesus comes again to claim His church. Who is the church? It is the people who have committed their lives to Him.

The foundation for spiritual growth is recognizing that it is

God who began a good work in you and He will one day bring it to completion – that is perfection. Our spiritual journey is rooted in what God *has* done, *is* doing and *will do* in our lives. He is working in our past, present and future and is faithful to continue. Therefore, you can trust that He will never let you go. He is in control.

And so, based on Philippians 1:6, can you achieve perfection in your life right now? No, you cannot, but you can *move* toward spiritual perfection by committing your life to Christ and living according to His will and purpose for you.

Trust Building Action

In the meantime, what are you to do until the day of Christ? Look again at Philippians 1:9–11 (HSCB).

> And I pray this: that your *love will keep on growing in knowledge and every kind of discernment*, so that you can approve the things that are superior and can *be pure and blameless* in the day of Christ, *filled with the fruit of righteousness* that comes through Jesus Christ to the glory and praise of God. [Emphasis added]

These verses are telling us to do three things until Jesus comes again:

1. *To love Him and His Word* in a way that we grow in knowledge and discernment and exhibit His love to others
2. *To be pure and blameless* – meaning to be cleansed from sin through prayer, confession and obedience to God. This does not mean instantaneous spiritual perfection, but rather an increasing likeness to Christ.
3. *To be filled with the fruit of righteousness* – this fruit is found in Galatians 5:22: Love, joy, peace, patience, kindness,

goodness, faith, gentleness, self-control. This fruit of the Spirit is not produced on our own.

The key to being able to do these things is found in Philippians 1:11 – "that comes through Jesus Christ to the glory and praise of God."

- How can you love Jesus and God's word if you don't know Him and have a personal relationship with Him?
- How can you be pure and blameless if you have not been washed clean by the Living Water who is Jesus?
- How can you be filled with the fruit of righteousness if you have not received the Holy Spirit by your faith in Christ?

The answer is you can't. These things can only be accomplished and received through Jesus Christ to the glory and praise of God. If you have not yet accepted Jesus as your personal Lord and Savior, now is the time. You will find a prayer to guide you in this decision at the end of this book.

Remember, part of the definition of *perfect* is sincere and blameless. The works of God *The* Rock are perfect! He wants you, whom He created, to strive toward sincerity and moral action. You are able because He is righteous and is working His righteousness in you.

Can you trust what He has written? We find the answer in Psalm 19.

> The instruction of the Lord is perfect renewing one's life; the testimony (*His story, His words*) of the Lord is trustworthy!
> Psalm 19:7 HCSB

Read how A. W. Tozer explains this in the following quote:

> *God is enthusiastic about His works. God is not an absentee engineer running His world by remote control. The Scripture says that He is "upholding all things by the word of his power." Hebrews 1:3, KJV. The presence of the invisible Word in the universe makes things run. God is the perfect creator and He runs everything by being present in His works.* – A. W. Tozer -[3]

Yes, God is the perfect creator running the world by being present. That is one of the many reasons why you can trust Him. He is the same for you today as He was at the time of creation. And, He is present at all times.

> *"God is the perfect creator and He runs everything by being present in His works."* – A. W. Tozer

Write, "The testimony of the Lord is trustworthy", from Psalm 19:7 on an index card. Put it somewhere you will see it every day until it resonates in your heart and mind that God is trustworthy. When that happens, He will be the first One you go to with your cares and difficulties. Trusting God when times are hard is not always easy. But He is trustworthy; therefore, you can trust Him.

Ask God to show you areas of your life where you are not flexible. Ask Him to help you allow Him to take control of everything about your life – especially the difficult circumstances you encounter along the way. God will turn your anxiety into peace as you ask Him to control your emotions.

I know He will answer that kind of prayer. He did it for me, and I am a more relaxed person because of His work in that area of my life. If you do something, or create something, that is not perfect according to man's standards, you can still be satisfied by trusting God in the details. He is in control and will guide you to the best solution for you. His works are perfect even when ours are not.

We can never make ourselves, or anyone else, perfect no matter how hard we try. God is the one who created us in His image, but the sin of the world has marred that perfection in us. Yet Jesus is without spot or blemish, and through Him, we are being made more and more into His spotless image as we trust Him with the details and difficulties of our lives. Then one day, when we meet Him face to face, we will be perfected in all His glory because we have trusted Him with our lives and with all our imperfections.

God created you for a relationship with Him. He did not create you so you would find something else to worship. He created you to worship Him. When you worship Him, the benefit is life–changing. When you love something you create more than God, it is all about you and the pride you have in what you have created. But when you love God with your whole being as the One who created you, it's all about Him and your relationship with Him. When life is lived all about God and a right relationship with Him, there is confidence. There is hope. There is satisfaction and fulfillment that cannot be achieved in anyone or anything else.

Yes, God intends for us to have relationships with people. There would be no point in staying on earth if that were not the case. I love my family. I love my friends. I even love people I do not know but have the opportunity to minister to. But relationships with people can be difficult. Do you know what I am talking about? The way to healthy relationships with people is to first have a healthy relationship with our Heavenly Father, to look first to Him for advice regarding your life and relationships. He is the One to worship. When our focus is redirected from the imperfection of people to the perfection of Jesus, there will be peace.

Questions for Personal Growth

- What about your life? Do you keep trying to become perfect?

- What changes in your thinking, if any, would help you to rest in God's perfection?

- What have you learned from the scriptures about trusting God with your imperfections?

Spend some time thinking about your priorities and asking God to help you put them in their proper order. He is the First and the Last, the Alpha and Omega.

It is through Jesus that we can be aware of changes needed in our thinking to be released from our need to be perfect so we can grow spiritually. This will happen as we develop a rock solid trust in Him.

CHAPTER 2
R.E.A.D. for Optional Study

Using the READ method of study, write your observations of the verse, example, application and direction for you from the scripture below.

He is The Rock – His works are perfect; and all His ways are just. A faithful God who does no wrong, upright and just is He.
Deuteronomy 32:4

R

E

A

D

CHAPTER 3

What's The Difference in a Word?

He is the Rock....
Deuteronomy 32:4

Words matter. Words make a difference in the meaning of other words. We find that in Deuteronomy 32 as Moses identified God as *The* Rock. The word *The* is *used as a function word to indicate that a following noun is a definite, unique and particular member of its class.*[4]

Understanding the difference between the Bible's use of *The* Rock and *a* rock becomes clear as you read this chapter. As you read Deuteronomy 32 in your Bible, circle each time you see Rock (with a capital R) and underline each time you see rock (with a small case r). What you will discover is that Moses is calling God *The Rock*. By using the word *The*, Moses is telling the children of Israel that God is the One and Only. There are no other gods before Him. He is definite. He is unique. He is the One and Only. He is the Rock of Israel. He is their strength and refuge.

However, the word 'a' is used as *a function word before singular nouns when the referent is unspecified such as 'a man overboard' and before number collectives and some numbers as a dozen.*[5] (Such as, one among many)

Virginia Grounds

But what do the differences in these two words (*the* and *a*) have to do with building your trust in God? Look through Deuteronomy 32:3–18, and place a checkmark above each description and phrase about God that can instill trust. How is He described that is still true for people today? You will also see the actions of those who turned away from God and how they are described. But even so, God is still The Rock. He is still the Most High, One and Only God. And He is still the Rock our Savior.

At the time of the Song of Moses written in Deuteronomy 32, there was a transition of leadership ready to take place. The people were in Moab before crossing over Jordan into Canaan. Moses' song was a warning to the people to get them on track for the future.

Throughout history, people have believed and rejected God, and yet, God never changes. He is the same yesterday, today and forever. What He says He will do, He does. That is something you can hang your hat on. He is trustworthy.

God created the human race to be His very own. In His commandments given on tablets to Moses, He very clearly stated, "Thou shall have no other gods before me." God knows us better than we know ourselves. He knew that ungodly celebration would result in ungodly deeds.

On the other hand, those who rejected God *The* Rock placed their trust in many rocks they called their gods. They deserted The Rock who fathered them and forgot all about Him. They acted corruptly toward God and sacrificed to demons. These were a people who were foolish and unwise – a warped and crooked generation indulging in sexual immorality with foreign women. As a result, they were influenced by a foreign way of worship, and bowed down to Baal in idol worship.[6]

It is a little eerie to read about the things the children of Israel in Moses' day were predicted to do, and are later revealed as truth. It is eerie because we see many of these things happening around us today. People worship many things, but not God. Sexual immorality is running rampant, which includes changing gender identity. We are being influenced by other religions to the point that Christianity is being watered down and persecuted. What grieves me most is the trend in public schools for accepting this behavior to the point of even rewarding the ungodly lifestyle of students for fear of reprimand or dismissal. Children are being taught to protest authority at home, in the schools, against government or anything that tells them they can't do something. We are living in an anything goes society. This is called *doing what is right in their own eyes*. There were consequences in the days of the Bible for that lifestyle, just as there are consequences today. People may not see the consequences in their lifetime, but a day will come when we all stand before God.

The Old Testament idols are described as having mouths but cannot speak, eyes but cannot see, ears but cannot hear, noses but cannot smell, hands but cannot feel, feet but cannot walk nor can they utter a sound with their throats.[7] Visible images are described that man created. So the question becomes, what purpose did they serve? I think the description speaks for itself. They served no purpose at all. These idols may be carved with human features, but just as they were useless in the days of the Bible, they are useless today.

However, in the New Testament, idols are described in Galatians 5 and Ephesians 5 as acts of a sinful nature and listed as immorality, impurity and greed among other things. In other words, in our current world, idolatry is not just the worship of created things, it is also *sinful acts* against your own body. Your body is the temple of the Holy Spirit, created to be holy, righteous and good. Therefore, it is to be treated as such.

The greedy want *things* more than they want God. The immoral and impure have excluded and rejected a relationship with God through Christ Jesus. They have turned to any person who they believe will fill the emptiness inside of them and give in to their demands. But there is only One who can fill the hole in our hearts, and that is Jesus. I know this personally because I spent miserable years looking for love in all the wrong places. Then I met Jesus and my life was changed forever, experiencing true love and peace for the first time in my life.

If you are a believer in Christ and, like me, came to know Him as an adult, you may have things in your past that relate to some areas of idolatry. You may have a family or friends who cannot accept the changes in you that came as a result of your salvation. However, you can know this. Godly living can bring persecution, but God provides a way for us to live in spite of it. It is easier to trust when you are a small child because of your innocence. It becomes more difficult as you grow older and have lived a lifestyle in complete contrast to the purity of Christ Jesus.

God is your faithful creator. It is arrogant and self-serving to trust in what you can make with your own hands. And yet, it is humbling to entrust your life to the One who created you. One of my favorite verses in the Bible is Ephesians 2:10 (NAS). "For we are God's workmanship created in Christ Jesus for good works..." Also 2 Timothy 2:15 (NAS); "Be diligent to present yourself to God as a workman who does not need to be ashamed, accurately handling the word of truth."

> "For we are God's workmanship created in Christ Jesus for good works..."
> Ephesians 2:10 (NAS).

Following the Song of Moses, he told Israel what to do to protect themselves from the influence of idols. He told them to "command your children to obey carefully all the words of this Law. They are not just idle words; they are your life. Take these words to heart." He was telling them that his message was a serious message of warning, to take them to heart and live by them.

So, the answer to *what's the difference in a word,* is God. He is the One and Only. He is not one of many gods created by man. He is the only One you can turn to for eternal salvation. He is the only One you can trust for your future. He is The One Rock, not one among many.

Trust Building Action

- *Acknowledge* that God is not *a* god among many gods. He is *The* One True God, the One and Only.
- *Accept* that God will one day perfect the work He began in you, and live toward that day by the fruit of the Spirit – love, joy, peace, patience, kindness, goodness, faithfulness, gentleness and self-control.
- *Allow* God, The Rock, to cleanse your heart and mind of the past so you can move forward toward the upward call of God in Christ Jesus. Confess your sin and weaknesses to Him. He will not only forgive you, He will carry you. He is strong enough to handle anything you throw His way.

Questions for Personal Growth

- In your own words, what is the difference in the word 'the' and the word 'a'?

- When referring to God, why do you think it is important to know the distinction in these two words?

- What consequences, if any, have you seen for those who trust in many things rather than the One True God?

- How does knowing there are consequences change your thinking toward who to trust?

CHAPTER 3
R.E.A.D. for Optional Study

Using the READ method of study, write your observations of the verse, example, application and direction for you from the scripture below.

> Do your best to present yourself to God
> as one approved, a worker
> who does not need to be ashamed, and
> who correctly handles the word of truth.
> 2 Timothy 2:15

R

E

A

D

CHAPTER 4

Trusting When Betrayed

*After saying these things, Jesus was
troubled in his spirit, and testified,
Truly, truly, I say to you, one of you will betray me.
John 13:21*

There was a time in my early twenties when I thought myself madly in love with a young man. We had a date on Tuesday before Thanksgiving that year, and he left on Wednesday to go on a ski trip with his buddies. He came back married!

I experienced shock and incredible pain and disbelief. Talk about betrayal! But it was that incident that drove me to move from a small Texas town to the big city of Dallas. And it was in Dallas where I came to know my Savior Jesus and where I met my husband.

I was not a believer when that happened, but I have learned that we experience the same painful emotions as believers when we feel betrayed. In fact, the pain is even worse when the interruption of betrayal comes from a believing brother or sister in Christ. My husband and I have experienced this kind of pain a few times throughout our lives and ministry. Betrayal hurts. It is unfaithful and disloyal. We have loved and trusted people who have later tried to discredit us, our faith, our ministry, and our testimony.

And since we are human, our first reaction to the shock and pain has been very human – to want to inflict pain in return or seek revenge. But each time, the Lord has very quickly captured our thoughts and shown us that the battle is His. He has delivered, will deliver and will continue to deliver us from these attempts to destroy what He has established in us and through us. (2 Corinthians 3:10) The Bible tells us in Romans that we are not to take revenge but to leave it to God. (Romans 12:19)

In one such spiritual battle, I felt pressed down and ineffective. Following the time of betrayal, I had been studying in Ephesians about putting on the armor of God. One thing I clung to is where it tells us that we are seated with Christ in the heavenly places. As I read that, I had an 'ah ha' moment – that if I am right there with Christ in the heavenly places, then I have access to see things from God's perspective. We are not to look at the disloyal person or what others may think as a result of the lies being spread, but we are to ask God to allow us to see the situation from His perspective and to show what our response is to be. In other words, trust God.

Is it easy? Of course not, but this one thing I know – when I respond according to my human nature, I am a miserable, distraught person. However, when I respond from God's perspective by the power of His Spirit, I am filled with His peace that is greater than any revenge could ever be. God's peace releases us from the anger, disappointment, pain and thoughts of how to get back at any person who betrays.

The bottom line is – God knows our pain. He is in control. He will do what He will do. It is not for us to determine the end result of betrayal, but to let go. That is what we have done in the past and, as a result, have seen God go before us and work things out in a way that clears the path for His purpose. I am so thankful we didn't miss the blessing by seeking our own revenge. Betrayal hurts, but God heals.

Paid to Betray

Even Jesus was betrayed by one of His very own – one who followed Him, ate with Him, prayed with Him and served with Him. Adding to the offence was the fact that Judas was paid to betray. The story of Judas is found in Matthew chapters 26–28. He sold out Jesus for thirty pieces of silver which, in today's economy, is equivalent to approximately a four-month salary. Think about it. Judas betrayed Jesus for the ability to live four months when he could have lived with Jesus for eternity by trusting Him and being faithful.

Jesus was sorrowful over what Judas was doing, but He realized it had to be done in order for His mission on earth to be complete. His mission was to sacrifice Himself in order to save people from sin and eternal separation from God.

Selfish Ambition Prompts Betrayal

Betrayal causes tremendous pain. But when the betrayer is one of your own, the pain is so deep and gut-wrenching, it is indescribable. Such was the case with King David. In the book of 2 Samuel Chapters 13–19 you find the tragic story of betrayal, conspiracy and murder – a story that takes your breath away. Let me give you a little background.

The story begins with three of David's grown children. Amnon, David's son, was obsessed with his sister Tamar. He devised a scheme in which he raped her in his bed chamber. Because of this, the other brother, Absalom, hated Amnon and devised a scheme leading to his murder.

In both of these situations, premeditation was involved. The rape and murder didn't just happen. They were planned. Betrayal is like that. Plans begin to take shape in the mind when anger, jealousy, selfish ambition, greed and lust for power take control of a life. That is what happened with the two sons of David. Amnon's lust for his sister betrayed the family. Absalom's revenge took the life of his brother. And so begins the story of betrayal in epic proportions.

When the news of his son's death reached David[8], he wept bitterly and mourned every day. But Absalom fled and was gone for three years. During this time, David had been comforted by the Lord and allowed Absalom to return to Jerusalem, but he would not see him for two more years. When he finally allowed his son to approach him, David forgave him and kissed him.

You would think this would be a happily ever after end of the story, but it is actually the beginning of a plot by Absalom to overthrow the King by turning people against him. The devastating betrayal of King David begins in the most painful way – when David's own son turned against him.

Betrayal is turning against others so you can take what is theirs for yourself. Betrayal is motivated by hate, greed, revenge and selfish ambition. Betrayal takes your kindness and forgiveness and uses it against you. That's what David's son did to him.

> *"Betrayal is turning against others so you can take what is theirs for yourself."*

In our generation, we read about, and possibly experience, this same type of betrayal. You may think it is new to this time in history, but you can see from David's story that it is not. Why? Why has this kind of behavior occurred throughout history? It is because of the selfish and greedy nature of mankind. It is because sin abounds. It is because man was not satisfied with what God had given into his care and took what was forbidden. Therefore, sin entered the world. The Devil spawned sin through deceit by tempting mankind to taste what was pleasing to the eye. You read all of this about Adam and Eve in the beautiful Garden of Eden God provided for them.[9]

The actions of Adam and Eve began the downward spiral of sin throughout the generations. What you find in the story of David and his children is sin in action. Tamar was appealing to the eyes of Amnon. This began a chain of events that movies are made of - sex, murder, betrayal and overthrow of power through manipulation. Therefore, a family was destroyed by betrayal.

In 2 Samuel 15, Absalom won the hearts of the people of David's kingdom. He was handsome, had beautiful hair, and was apparently charming, as he convinced people at the gate of the city that he was a better man of justice than his father. How they could believe this after all he had done is beyond me. Talk about crooked politics and split loyalties! But the day came when a messenger came to David and said "the hearts of the men of Israel are with Absalom." As a result, King David and his followers were forced to flee. And David wept.

The word betrayal as a noun is defined as *disloyal, treachery, deception, double-cross, stab in the back* and *breach of faith*. The word betray as a verb is defined as *delivering into the hands of the enemy, to desert in time of need*.[10]

And so, there you have it – betrayal of the worst kind. It is not pretty. If you have ever felt betrayed, I am sure you can relate to David in his grief. It also shows us that family dysfunction is not new to our generation. But there are things we can learn from David's story for our response to those who betray us.

First read Psalm 3, David's prayer as he fled. In fact, 2 Samuel 15:30 says this: "David continued up the Mount of Olives, weeping as he went…" It makes me wonder if this was the place he voiced the prayer of Psalm 3.

> LORD, how my foes increase! There are many who attack me.
> Many say about me, 'There is no help for him in God.'
> But you, LORD are a shield around me,
> My glory, and the one who lifts up my head.

> I cry aloud to the LORD, and He answers me from
> His holy mountain.
> I lie down and sleep; I wake again because the
> LORD sustains me.
> I will not be afraid of thousands of people
> Who have taken their stand against me on every
> side.
> Rise up, LORD! Save me, my God!
> You strike all my enemies on the cheek; You break
> the teeth of the wicked.
> Salvation belongs to the LORD; may your blessing
> be on your people.
> Psalm 3 HCSB

Can you see the problem? Betrayal is never satisfied alone. Betrayal gets others to join in through lies and manipulation, and therefore, foes increase. People begin to notice and say that God cannot help you. When you begin to see others pulling away from you, it is so easy to fall into despair. It is easy to have a great big pity party and isolate yourself from embarrassment.

Yes, David wept and fled. But even in doing so, *he still trusted God.* He still acknowledged God as surrounding Him with protection and lifting his head from the pain of betrayal. He acknowledged God as his only salvation even when others said God would not save him. David knew differently because of his faith and rock solid trust. Therefore, David turned to God. He trusted God to do what man could not.

He claimed God as his shield. A shield is a cover or barrier that protects or defends. A warrior's shield is carried in front of him, but God as our Shield *surrounds* us. His protection and defense is all around us. Knowing this strengthens our trust. He is not just carried on our arm as a protective barrier, but is everywhere present. If you go forward, He is there. If you look behind, He is there. If you turn to the left or right, He is there – guiding you in the way you should go.

Two Sides of Betrayal

You find a similarity in reading about the betrayals of Jesus and David. And yet, there are differences in the end result. Absalom and Judas were both motived by greed. Judas was after money. Absalom wanted power. In the betrayal of Jesus, there was a purpose carried out to fulfill the way of the cross. It had to be done for the atonement of sin once for all. Don't misunderstand: God was *not* the betrayer. He knew Satan's character and how He would use the evil actions through Judas.

God *did*, however, *use* the greed of Judas to carry out the plan for our salvation through Jesus' shed blood on the cross.

But the enemy was at work in the betrayal of David by his son to destroy a kingdom established by God. Absalom betrayed his father for his own selfish ambition and gain of power. It was all about him with no regard to God's plan and purpose for David.

Satan is still at work today to destroy lives, families and the Kingdom of God. What gives me peace is in recognizing that God sees it all, hears it all and knows it all. He will accomplish His purpose. When we trust God with the end result rather than seeking revenge, He can, and will, take what man meant for evil and use it for our good.

Trust Building Action

Read Psalm 3 again and write your observations to the following:

- What was the problem?

- What did others say about him?

- What was David's response?

- How is God described?

- What was the action of God David proclaimed?

Questions for Personal Growth:

- Have you ever felt betrayed by someone close to you?

- How did you feel?

- How did you respond?

- What can you learn from David in how to respond to personal betrayal?

To help strengthen your trust in God, pray as David did. Claim these promises of God.

> But let all who take refuge in you rejoice;
> Let them shout for joy forever.
> May you shelter them,
> And may those who love your name boast about you.
> For you, LORD, bless the righteous one;
> You surround him with favor like a shield.
> Psalm 5:11–12 HCSB

CHAPTER 4
R.E.A.D. for Optional Study

Using the READ method of study, write your observations of the verse, example, application and direction for you from the scripture below.

> But let all who take refuge in you rejoice;
> Let them shout for joy forever.
> May you shelter them,
> And may those who love your name boast about you.
> For you, LORD, bless the righteous one;
> You surround him with favor like a shield.
> Psalm 5:11–12 HCSB

R

E

A

D

CHAPTER 5

Trusting When Exhausted

*Come to me, all you who are weary and burdened,
and I will give you rest.*
Matthew 11:28

End-of-the-day exhaustion is different than bone-weary exhaustion from an extended period of events. These events can be good, even ministry related, or they can be unhappy, difficult situations. The result is the same when there is no time of rest. Even while writing this book, I became so consumed with writing that time slipped away. One day I realized I hadn't been out of the house in three weeks! It was taking a toll on my physical and mental state. I needed to withdraw for a while. The body and mind need rest and time away from that which drains our energy, even if it is a good thing.

Such was the case with King David. He was following God's commands, but He became battle weary. His leadership team recognized his need for rest and protection and told him to withdraw from battle. From the time he defeated Goliath, a Philistine, as a youth, he fought battles with the Philistines time after time. But no one can fight battle after battle without becoming exhausted.

> The Philistines again waged war against Israel. David went down with his soldiers, and they fought the Philistines, but David became exhausted.
> 2 Samuel 21:15 HCSB

At this point in David's life, he had been fighting battles approximately thirty-eight years from the time of slaying Goliath. This would make him about fifty-five years of age. No wonder he was tired!

This shows us that even the godly have occasions in life when they face the same old battles over and over again. I think you would agree that fighting the same problems, the same situations, and the same people repeatedly is very exhausting. It does wear you down. Fighting can drag you into a downward spiral unless there is a season of rest and refreshing of the soul.

For twenty years as a chaplain, my husband responded to victims of crime and disaster following events that left people traumatized. If there was time and space between each response, he could remain prayed up and mission ready. But if the responses were one on top of another for an extended period of time, he became exhausted physically, emotionally and spiritually. In the beginning of his ministry, he could withstand the pressure for longer periods of time. He was younger then. But as years went by without a break, exhaustion was a constant battle. He needed rest.

When a person is in this condition, they cannot be effective in their mission. Such was the case with David when a descendent of the giant tried to kill him. His men strongly encouraged him to hang up his fighting clothes and never go into battle again. They told him, "You must not extinguish the lamp of Israel" (2 Samuel 21:17b HCSB).

In other words, the King of Israel must be protected. He exposed himself to death each time he entered into battle in a state of fatigue. He needed rest in order to lead effectively.

We don't always recognize the need to take time away from what we are doing, especially if it is something we know God has called us to do. But those close to us will recognize our need. When they point out to us that it is time to stop and rest, we need to listen.

The Song of David in 2 Samuel 22 is a description of battles fought and God's deliverance. It is similar to the Song of Moses from Deuteronomy 32 in many ways. The message given is you *can* trust God even when times are hard. You *can* trust God when you are betrayed. You *can* trust God when you are exhausted. What you find with David and Moses is God's deliverance and their trust in Him through every battle and difficulty.

> The Lord is *my* rock, *my* fortress,
> and *my* deliverer, *my* God,
> *my* rock in whom I seek refuge [emphasis added]."
> 2 Samuel 22:2–3a HCSB

Moses and David both refer to God as *rock,* meaning He is solid and unbreakable. However, Moses said, God *THE* Rock" [emphasis added], meaning the one and only. But David said, "The Lord is MY Rock [emphasis added]". David made it personal.

What this means for you and me is that God is the One and Only God, but even so, He is still very personal for those who know Him and place their trust in Him.

> My God, my mountain where I seek refuge. My shield, the horn of my salvation, my stronghold, my refuge, and my Savior, You save me from violence. I called to the Lord who is worthy of praise, and I was saved from my enemies.
> 2 Samuel 22: 3–4 HCSB

Another similarity is found in verses 31–32. David said, "God – His way is perfect; the word of the Lord is pure. He is a shield to all who take refuge in Him. For who is God besides the Lord? And who is a rock? Only our God".

Rock Solid Trust

Moses said God's *work* is perfect – that is His creation. But David said, His *way* is perfect. We see the perfection of God in His creation and in His direction. God will never direct us to go outside the path He has chosen for us. His *way* of living is perfect.

David said, "God is my strong refuge; He makes *my* way perfect [emphasis added]. He makes my feet like the feet of a deer and sets me securely on the heights" (2 Samuel 22:31–34 HCSB).

Not only is God's way perfect, but he points us in the right direction for the safety, security and rest needed from difficult circumstances causing exhaustion. If you are tempted in a direction that does not line up with the Word of God, then He is *not* the one doing the leading. He will never lead you where His Word does not tell you to go. He will lead you in His perfect way.

I am sure you know what it means to feel exhausted, but the dictionary describes it like this: *drawn out, drained off, emptied, draining or evaporation, wholly used or expended, consumed.*

Yes, I can relate to all of that, can't you? Drained, empty, stretched beyond what you are able, all used up, and feeling as if you have nothing left to give. If someone asks one more thing of you, you just want to run away screaming.

The word is not only used to describe David, but also Gideon, his army, young men, Israel in the desert, Job, the disciples and Paul. It is used to describe both the righteous and unrighteous.

Exhaustion is a condition that can apply to anyone when exertion becomes excessive. But the good news is this - *our exhaustion is God's opportunity.* He uses it to teach us and to give us a testimony of His strength and faithfulness. In our weakness, He is *always* strong. And so doesn't it make sense to trust Him with our weaknesses?

> "Our exhaustion is God's opportunity."

Just as exhaustion is God's opportunity, it is also an open door for attacks on our soul by the enemy who wants to destroy our faith in God. Satan uses the opportunity of our exhaustion to throw temptations our way. The temptation to give up on life, to give up on God, to seek revenge and to go a different way than God's perfect way.

This is the spiritual battle we face time after time. We get so tired of fighting that in our weakness of exhaustion, we just want to stay in bed with the covers over our head. But let me say to you again – God's way is perfect and His Word proves true. He will always make a way for you when there seems to be no way.

The following is a text I received that tells how God led the way to rest for one who was weary and in need of refreshing.

> *Hey Ladies. I have an awesome God story to share with you today. It's just amazing how He knows exactly what we need and when we need it.*
>
> *I'm having a very rough morning and am struggling with some stuff at work that makes me very anxious. So I went to see my friend for a minute to "vent" and get some stuff off my chest. She's my safe harbor here at work. But she wasn't around. So I really needed to get away from my 4th floor people so that I would not blow up at anyone. I went down to the 3rd floor to just sit and catch my breath a minute. I decided to go see a friend on that floor just to kill a few minutes and gather myself. I've never just shown up at her desk before unless it was specifically work related. When I sat down at her desk, I just said I was taking a time out and had been having a very rough morning.*
>
> *She had a piece of paper and some scissors in her hand. She had just printed out a prayer with fancy letters and a pretty border. Two of them fit on the piece of paper. So she was cutting the first one out and trimming it down*

to size to tape to her computer. She just happened to have that second one that had printed out on her sheet. She didn't know why she printed two! She just did. Of course, I showed up right at that moment, anxious and in need.

She may have seen this prayer somewhere or written it herself, I have no idea, but God delivered it to me today right when I needed it!!

Dear Lord, Thank you for lifting me out of this pit time and time again. Forgive me of my doubt and lack of faith when storms hit. Strengthen me and remind me of your faithfulness! Thank you for providing a firm foundation for my feet. Guide me as I go through each day to stay on the path you have laid out for me helping me to avoid the hidden pits dug out by my enemy. In Jesus' holy name. Amen!

So hallelujah, praise His holy name. I got chills. I know it's just a small thing but that almost makes it even more awesome. He's not just watching my major struggles. But He's also here for the day to day stuff that chips away at our souls little by little. I feel so fortified today and I just wanted to share that with you. She also said she's been praying for me all morning. – Deanna –

You see, God's way is perfect. The temptation was there for her to blow up at her co-workers and she knew it. But God, whose way is perfect, directed her to a place of refuge where she would hear a word from Him.

Trust Building Action

We always have a choice in our exhaustion, our frustration and our rough mornings. But God...

- Whose *works* are perfect – that is you in creation.
- Whose *way* is perfect – this is the direction given you to follow Him.

He is always the right choice! You may be looking for what you consider to be a safe harbor in people, but God will lead you to the place and person He will use when needed as your safe harbor. He is your refuge, a very present help in time of trouble. He will not lead you astray because He is trustworthy.

It is the Lord who saves in the battle. David knocked down a giant with trust in God and a stone. His message to the giant was, "You come to me with a sword, a spear and with a javelin, but I come to you in the name of the Lord of hosts, the God of the armies of Israel, whom you have defied. Today, the Lord will hand you over to me ... Then all the world will know that Israel has a God, and this whole assembly will know that it is not by sword or by spear that the Lord saves, *for the battle is the Lord's* [emphasis added]. He will hand you over to us." (1 Samuel 17:45–47 NAS)

You can knock down the giants in your life with trust in God and a prayer. The battle is not yours, but the Lord's.

Make the choice to turn your battles over to him. He will go before you to pave the way. Do as David did when exhausted, turn to the Lord your God. God gave him rest, and He will do the same for you.

A few definitions of the word 'rest' from the Bible are to *'settle down, be quiet, withdraw, given comfort, cease and to draw breath.'*[11] Additional meanings signify *'to cause or permit one to cease from any labor or movement so as to recover strength. It implies previous toil and* care.'[12] But the definition that I love from the same source says, 'to give intermission from labor'.

Read the following verses and write what you learn about God's part in our rest.

- Exodus 33:14

- Matthew 11:28

Questions for Personal Growth

- What has exhausted you?

- What battles are you facing?

- Think about the phrase *to give intermission*. What does the word intermission mean to you? How can you give it to yourself?

- How can you apply what you have read to your personal circumstances in a way that gives you relief?

Read the words of Jesus and allow them to encourage you today.

> Come to Me, all you who are weary and burdened,
> and I will give you rest.
> Matthew 11:28

CHAPTER 5

R.E.A.D. for Optional Study

Using the READ method of study, write your observations of the verse, example, application and direction for you from the scripture below.

> Come to Me, all you who are weary and burdened,
> and I will give you rest.
> Matthew 11:28

R

E

A

D

CHAPTER 6

Trust Even When Threatened

*For the Lord your God is the one who goes with you
to fight for you against your enemies to give you victory.
Deuteronomy 20:4*

In a battle, there are winners and there are losers. You may think, how can I be a winner without a fight? David trusted the Lord his God when faced with insurmountable odds. You can too.

There have been so many storms that have affected our nation over the last decade. The ones in particular that caught my attention were the tornadoes, hurricanes and flooding. There was a story on the news about a car that had overturned and was lying upside down in the sweeping floodwaters. People were rushing into the water trying to stop the car from being swept away as they checked inside for victims. They found two babies strapped in their car seats in the back and struggled to remove them. The younger of the two was not breathing. A man finally had the car seat and was struggling to get it to safety. Once there, he began CPR. He worked and worked and worked, but nothing was happening.

Someone was using their cell phone to show all of this and in the background you could hear a woman crying out to the Lord asking Him to breathe his breath into this baby. She just kept saying over and over give this baby breath Lord. Give him breath, and breathe your breath into this baby. Then, suddenly, the man raised his head and said, "I got him back." You could hear the woman then praising Jesus saying "Thank you Jesus, thank you Lord."

There were many good Samaritans there that day. The article was touting this man as a hero, and yes he was a hero. He is the one who dragged the baby from the car, he is the one that performed CPR on her and he's the one whom God used to breathe the breath of life into the baby.

But I believe there was another hero there that day, one who will probably remain unknown. I believe it was the woman standing on the sidelines in the background praying, crying out to God to breathe the breath of life into the baby and to save his life. This was a woman who knew where to turn when a battle was being fought for life.

You begin to realize the effectiveness of prayer and praise as you prepare to face battles in your life through this real life example; the spiritual battles we face on a day-to-day basis. Then you can read about a perfect Biblical example of how to prepare for, and face, battles in the book of 2 Chronicles in the life of King Jehoshaphat.

How can you be a winner without a fight? What does it mean to be threatened? The word threatened means *'to cause someone or something to be vulnerable or at risk; endanger,* as was the case with the lives of the storm victims. It also means *'to state one's intention to take hostile action against someone in retribution for something done or not done'*[13] as is the case with King Jehoshaphat that you find in 2 Chronicles 20. The chapter begins like this:

> After this, the Moabites and Ammonites with some
> of the Meunites came to make war on Jehoshaphat.
> 2 Chronicles 20:1

But as you will see, King Jehoshaphat is a king who won the battle against three armies without ever lifting his sword. This is one of my favorite passages of scripture because it gives us clear guidance for how to respond when we feel threatened in any way. The enemy we face today is an unseen supernatural force, but his threats are very real. We may not be facing three armies at the same time in the physical sense, but we can certainly face three threats to our personal lives at the same time from spiritual warfare.

And so, the same principles of response we read about in 2 Chronicles 20 can be applied to our personal lives when something or someone is coming against us to destroy our integrity, our marriage, our family, our health, our career or anything else.

The threat was described in Verse 1 followed by the report to the king in Verse 2. "Some people came and told Jehoshaphat, 'A vast army is coming against you from Edom from the other side of the Dead Sea. It is already in En Gehi."

Immediate insight into the character of this king is found in Verse 3. It tells us the first thing he did when he heard the news was to inquire of the Lord and call a fast. In other words, he immediately asked the Lord what his response was to be to this threat.

We can learn a very important lesson from this example. So often we want to charge headlong into a situation without thought or preparation. But the first thing we learn to do here is to stop and ask for God's wisdom and direction.

Of course, we don't always have warning before a threat is a reality, as was the case of the overturned car in a storm. But in day to day situations, taking time to ask God's direction is a must for survival.

What threats can you think of that face our generation? Are you facing any personal threats against you?

Terrorism, disasters, watered down faith or no faith, our liberties and freedom threatened, human trafficking, mass shootings, and much dissention among opposing sides politically are a few threats faced in this generation. The most heartbreaking is the attack of the enemy on our teenagers and children. They are being exposed to lies about their identity. They are taking guns to school to resolve their differences. Young lives are being taken too early as a result of violence. Respect is gone and replaced with rebellion. The freedom of the Christian faith is under attack such as we have not seen before.

But the Bible warns us that these things will take place as the day draws near for the return of Christ.

> People will be lovers of themselves, lovers of money, boastful, proud, abusive, disobedient to their parents, ungrateful, unholy, without love, unforgiving, slanderous, without self-control, brutal, not lovers of the good, treacherous, rash, conceited, lovers of pleasure rather than lovers of God— having a form of godliness but denying its power. Have nothing to do with such people.
> 2 Timothy 3:2

From 2 Chronicles 20:1-2, you find that three armies were coming against Judah at the same time. They were uniting in the cause to wipe out the Israelites. How can you relate to something of this magnitude? I can tell you from personal experience there was a time when our family faced three difficulties at the same time. The enemy of our soul tried to drag us into defeat and despair through the circumstances. But praise God the enemy was defeated. This reveals that just as the enemy came against Judah, the enemy is still at work to destroy the lives of people robbing them of peace, health and trust. Just as a Godly pattern of response worked in Jehoshaphat's life, it can work for you.

It is difficult to know what to say to someone who has faced threats resulting in loss of life as occurred in recent school shootings. What do you tell parents who sent their teenager to school where they faced the threat of death? What do you tell the parents whose child didn't come home. Those are tough questions. Sometimes it is best not to say anything immediately following the loss. However, it is important to show continual support and concern in tangible ways to be Jesus in skin. Be someone present and a listening ear. Show compassion. Give a hug. They may need to rant in anger. Just listen with a sympathetic ear.

Trauma is a threat to children, including teens, turning their lives upside down. To them, the trauma becomes like an ongoing, festering splinter that keeps hurting. This threat sends four messages:

- Your world is no longer safe.
- Your world is no longer kind.
- Your world is no longer predictable.
- Your world is no longer trustworthy.

When this happens, they are in danger of becoming impaired emotionally all the way into adulthood. In the first state of their crisis, there will be shock followed by anxiety. Feeling helpless to save others in the situation will develop into feelings of guilt.[14] It is important to allow the person traumatized to talk out their feelings. I have heard it said, *what they don't talk out, they will act out*. Those four fears can be resolved with the help of God, the One who is trustworthy.

> But he who trusts in the LORD, mercy shall surround him.
> Psalm 32:10b, NKJV

King Jehoshaphat prepared a divine defense. What we see with him are *preventative* measures. Senior Pastor of Prestonwood Baptist Church, Dr. Jack Graham, addressed this as application for our lives when faced with a fight:

> *"We must prepare a divine defense to win the battle God has called us to fight." - Dr. Jack Graham*

"We must prepare a divine defense to win the battle God has called us to fight." [15]

Following the king's example from 2 Chronicles 20:1–2, what you can do when you are faced with threats is to seek the counsel of the Lord. Somehow in the middle of trauma and loss, He will provide wisdom through His word, His Spirit and prayer, and will often use others or something you may see or read to clarify your decisions and the path you are to take.

Jesus tells us in Matthew 6:33 to "Seek first His Kingdom and His righteous and all these things will be added to you." Seek Him first before any preparations, before any decisions, before any action. Seek Him first. And you are promised in His Word that when you seek God with all your heart, you will find Him. (Jeremiah 29:13)

There may be times when you are faced with threats, challenges or difficult decisions that you want to seek advice from the ungodly rather than inquiring of the Lord. You just want to hear from anyone who will listen to your plea. But the Bible is very clear on this subject.

> When someone tells you to consult mediums and spiritists, who whisper and mutter, should not a people inquire of their God? Why consult the dead on behalf of the living? Consult God's instruction and the testimony of warning. If anyone does not speak according to this word, they have no light of dawn.
> Isaiah 8:19–20

In other words, if the wisdom through others is not from God, it is no wisdom at all. If it is a fortune-teller or horoscope, it is not God's wisdom. It does not shed the light of His direction in your life. If you pray asking God for direction, don't go to those who do not know Him. Don't listen to or follow their advice. Their words

Virginia Grounds

are not directed by the Lord, but rather by their own knowledge and opinions.

King Jehoshaphat trusted God when he was threatened by not one, not two, but three armies coming against him at the same time. His story shows us that even godly leaders can have circumstances of facing threats from the enemy. But the way he handled his threat was to completely trust and obey the Lord.

It takes strong faith and courage to face the challenges of life. But we simply cannot defeat the enemy and win any battles in life without having a rock solid trust in our God and Savior, Jesus Christ. He makes a way when there seems to be no way. Our part in all difficulties is to follow Him, to trust Him, to go where He leads in complete obedience.

The first thing the king did when Judah was threatened by three armies was to *inquire of the Lord*. His trust was so rock solid that he knew he could not face this threat without direction from God. And so He prayed and in his prayer, he made commitments to God.

> If disaster comes upon us – sword, judgment, pestilence, or famine – we will stand before this temple and in your presence and cry out to you in our affliction, and you will hear and save.
> 2 Chronicles 20:9 NKJV

> O our God, will you not judge them? For we have no power against this great multitude that is coming against us; nor do we know what to do, *but our eyes are upon you*. [Emphasis added].
> 2 Chronicles 20:12 NKJV

Have you faced a situation where you were simply without answers, and you didn't know what to do? This king made three commitments:

1. To stand in the presence of God (take refuge in Him)
2. To cry out to God (Psalm 34:15) – "The eyes of the Lord are on the righteous and His ears are attentive to their cry".
3. To keep his eyes on God (to watch in hope as I wait for God to answer)

> It is better to take refuge in the LORD than to trust in humans. It is better to take refuge in the LORD than to trust in princes.
> Psalm 118:8–9

Trust Building Action

We often go to others for advice and trust them to take care of our circumstances, but it is God whom we are to trust with everything. Our confidence comes from keeping our eyes on Jesus. What happens when we keep our eyes on Him? Read the following verses and underline the benefit to you for keeping your eyes on Jesus:

- Psalm 34:5 – Those who look to Him are radiant; their faces are never put to shame.
- Isaiah 26:3 – You will keep in perfect peace him whose mind is steadfast because he trusts in you.
- Psalm 105:3-4 – Let the hearts of those who seek the Lord rejoice.
- Jeremiah 6:16 – Walk in the good way and you will find rest for your souls.
- John 1:29 – The Lamb of God who takes away the sins of the world.

God's eyes are always on you. He hears when you cry out to

Him with your troubles. Back in the days of the Bible, people were still worshiping wooden idols. They were made with eyes that could not see and ears that could not hear. The Lord our God can see and He can hear. He came to earth in the form of man – flesh and blood, that we would know Him. His eyes are on us and He knows our needs. As we trust Him with those needs and praise Him, we may have to wait for an answer in a timeframe not our own, but He will answer. He will meet all our needs in Christ Jesus.

King Jehoshaphat made commitments to his Lord. Jehoshaphat prayed a beautiful prayer when faced with difficulty. He gathered all the people together to join him in prayer. In this prayer, he acknowledged the sovereignty of God and committed to stand before Him, to cry out to Him and to keep his eyes on God in the midst of these life-threatening circumstances. To describe his prayer and commitment in a word is trust! He was saying to God, I trust you no matter what.

I wonder if you can say the same thing. If destructive forces are on their way to you, and you know they are coming, will you trust God with the circumstances and the result? Will you praise Him while moving forward toward the difficulty? That is not an easy thing to do. But there is so much encouragement and wisdom to be learned from Jehoshaphat's prayer and response.

Just as King Jehoshaphat did, plant these steps in your heart and mind putting them to practice the moment you feel threatened and have that first inkling of fear:

- Turn your attention to *seek the Lord*
- *Fast*
- *Pray* acknowledging God's sovereignty
- Pray making your *commitments to God*
- *Stand* before Him
- *Cry out to Him* in your distress
- When you don't know what to do, *keep your eyes on the Lord*
- *Sing praise to God* while moving forward

All of this equals trust. This is how you trust in the relationship you have with the Lord Jesus.

God's response to this kind of trust in Him is found in 2 Chronicles 20:14–19. Read these verses in your Bible in order to answer the questions for personal growth.

Questions for Personal Growth:

God first addressed their fear and discouragement. Based on trusting God, answer the following questions.

- Are you facing any threats right now?

- How do you typically react, or respond, to threats? What is the difference between *react* and *respond*?

- What have you learned from this chapter to help you prepare for future threats?

- Think about some challenge you have faced that required a fight to win. Did you trust in your ability to win the fight or did you trust God to fight for you?

What we learn from this is that instead of retaliation, we are to rest in Him. He knows what is happening. He will do what is best.

- In 2 Chronicles 20:16–17, what assurance and instruction did God give?

Go forward. You will not have to fight this battle. Take your position, stand firm, see the deliverance the Lord will give you. Do not be afraid, do not be discouraged. Go out and face them and the Lord will be with you.

- What was the king's response from verses 18–19?

He bowed with his face to the ground and all the people worshiped the Lord. God encouraged the people of Judah by claiming the battle as His own. But He also gave instruction for them to follow. King Jehoshaphat's response was obedience. He led by example and instruction to the people.

As he did, a miracle occurred. The people went before the army singing praise to the Lord and as the army approached the battlefield, what did they find? There was no battle to fight! The Lord had gone before them and fought the battle. Theirs was a victory without a fight because they fully trusted God and did all He said in preparation for facing the battle.

This story from the Bible is a picture of spiritual battle. It was real then. It is real now. We face spiritual battles more and more as the day draws near for the return of Christ.

From their response as they marched toward the battle, we can learn how to approach any difficulties we face. We learn that God goes before us when the enemy is fighting to destroy our faith. We learn to sing praise to God on our way to face a threat.

Make it a habit to sing songs of the faith that praise the name of Jesus, trusting that He has gone ahead to make a way for victory. Download songs to listen to throughout the day that teach God's Word and lift you up in encouragement.

He is faithful.

Therefore, from David and Jehoshaphat, we learn to:

- *Move forward* when God says go
- *Withdraw* when He says no
- *Trust Him* to fight your battles for you.

God said "You will not have to fight this battle. Take your position, stand firm, see the deliverance the Lord will give you. Do not be afraid, do not be discouraged. Go out and face them, the Lord will be with you" (2 Chronicles 20:16–17 NKJV).

God's Word from this verse is two-fold. He promised deliverance for His people, and He promised to be present with them as they forged ahead. Do you understand that both of these promises are yours to claim? God is with you to deliver as you face potential battles. He will deliver in His way and in His time. Just trust. He wants you to be prepared, and to act upon your faith, but He is with you all the way.

What a great encouragement we have in the example of King Jehoshaphat. If you are facing potentially devastating circumstances, God says face tomorrow with faith and trust in Him. You have a promise from His word that He will fight for you. But the first thing to do in order to move forward with hope and healing is to pray, acknowledge the problem, and ask God to work in it. Then worship His Holy Name and sing praises to Him. As you praise Him, you can know that He is in the midst of your battle making a way for

Virginia Grounds

your tomorrow whether it be a battle of emotions or relationships or something else. He wants you to do something, face it, move forward and receive the blessings of obedience He has for you.

Read Psalm 31 and make it your prayer today.

CHAPTER 6
R.E.A.D. for Optional Study

Using the READ method of study, write your observations of the verse, example, application and direction for you from the scripture below.

> For the Lord your God
> is the one who goes with you
> to fight for you against your enemies
> to give you victory.
> Deuteronomy 20:4

R

E

A

D

CHAPTER 7

Trusting Where God Leads

> The Lord had said to Abram, 'Leave your country,
> Your people and your father's household
> And go to the land I will show you'.
> Genesis 12:1

I love roads. I don't know why, I just do. The more they wind and turn, the better I like them. Call me crazy, but I think a road with texture and curves is beautiful! It must be the thought of going places, but not being able to see where that draws me forward. It reminds me of Abram's journey in the Bible of going without knowing where. All he knew was that God told him to go to a place He would show him. So he followed the direction of the Lord.

Life is like that. No matter how well we plan for the future, no one really knows all the bends, bumps or rocky terrain we will face in the road along the way. Life is a journey, but it is the unexpected around the bend that keeps us alert with anticipation and pressing on over the rough, rocky places. A winding road that we have never traveled before presents the opportunity for something new and exciting, even if it does not seem like it at the present time. The following quote is a statement worth remembering.

Rock Solid Trust

"God never said that the journey would be easy, but He did say that the arrival would be worth the trip." – Max Lucado -

Christopher Columbus was the explorer credited with the discovery of America. His journey was certainly not easy, but definitely worth the trip. After seven years of trying to convince the monarchs of Europe to finance his expedition, he finally won the support of Queen Isabella of Castille and King Ferdinand of Aragon. Columbus set sail on August 3, 1492, and after the longest voyage ever made out of sight of land, discovered the New World on October 12, 1492.

> "God never said that the journey would be easy, but He did say that the arrival would be worth the trip." – Max Lucado

The writings from his journal prove him to be a man of God who trusted God every wave of the journey through the seas. Queen Isabella's commission to Columbus was this: *"It is hoped that by God's assistance some of the continents and islands in the ocean will be discovered…for the glory of God."* His goal then, was to go and discover other continents and islands *for the glory of God.*

His journal also stated that he had previously depended upon his learning and navigational skills in his expeditions, but in setting out for the New World, his journey was totally dependent upon the leadership of God.[16]

In traveling our journeys, the Bible teaches that we are to seek direction from the Lord for every twist, turn and fork in the road we face. We've each been given a journey to travel in this life we live on our way to a future orchestrated by God.

But often, we make our plans without seeking the Lord's direction. When we do that, we are opening the door to a path we were not meant to follow.

Abram, a man from the days of the Old Testament, had lived in the same place all his life until the Lord moved him. The Bible tells us that "the Lord said to Abram, 'Leave your country, your people and your father's household and go to the land I will show you'" (Genesis 12:1).

So, at seventy-five years of age, Abram left as the Lord had instructed him. He was to go to a place he had never been, but he was obedient, trusting in the wisdom of God.

Was it easy to leave his homeland behind and the people he had known all his life? No, he had many hardships along the way. But with those difficulties came the blessings of God as He provided, protected and led him to a land He promised. Abram went with trust and confidence that no matter what happened, God would be with him and God would bless him because He promised He would.

I'm sure Abram had many questions, but he went anyway, trusting God for the answers to be revealed when the time was right.

Perhaps you have many questions right now in a situation that is very difficult to understand, and even though there are not answers in this moment, there is direction. The direction for you is the same as it was for Abram long, long ago – that direction is simply to do the next thing trusting God in the process.

Abram didn't know where he was going or how long he would be there, but when he was told to go, he did the next thing. He packed up and made himself ready for the journey, trusting God for the end result. All along the way he didn't know what tomorrow would bring, but he did the next thing that would carry him further into the journey. When trouble blocked his way, he did the next thing and listened to direction from God.

As you travel your journey without knowing what the future holds, God has a word for you.

> Fear not, for I am with you; do not be dismayed, for I am your God. I will strengthen you, yes, I will help you; I will uphold you with my righteous right hand.
> Isaiah 41:10 NKJV

Abram, whose name was later changed to Abraham, was obedient to follow God's plan and direction when he was told to leave his home and all he was familiar with, but there came a day in his travels when he made a decision on his own. When preparing to cross the border into Egypt, Abraham lied about his wife Sarah and said she was his sister because he feared for his safety. This led to all kinds of problems when Pharaoh took her into his home not knowing she was married. In addition, when God told Abram to leave his land and family, he took family with him. This led to problems when his nephew Lot chose to live in Sodom and Gomorrah.

The Bible is very clear about the plans of man versus the plans of God. When we try to add to God's plan or change it in any way, there will always be problems. And with problems there are consequences. The book of Proverbs is filled with wisdom on this subject. Read these verses from the Holman Christian Standard Bible translation.

Proverbs 15:22 – "Plans fail when there is no counsel, but with many advisers they succeed".

The word counsel in this verse means *"to circle together in assembly and intimacy with God.* In other words, plans succeed as you come together with others, seeking direction from the Lord. Seeking Him first is the way to agreement.

Proverbs 15:26 – "The Lord detests the plans of an evil man, but pleasant words are pure".

The evil man is obviously in reference to the ungodly. Your direction will never be clear and your plans may fail when following the evil devices of the ungodly. However, conversations spiced with pleasant, kind, and gracious words are pleasing to the Lord

Proverbs 16:2 – "All a man's ways seem right to him, but the Lord evaluates the motives".

This is interesting. The word *motives,* in part, means *spirit, breath of the mouth, of will and counsel.*[17] I never really thought about our motives being revealed through what comes out of our mouth, but that is what it means. If we allow the Spirit to evaluate our motives before we speak, our words will be filtered before they are spoken. In addition, the Lord evaluates the seat of your moral character for the plans you make. He knows if your plans are motivated for your own benefit, or for the benefit of others to glorify God. Therefore, if we allow our motives to be controlled by the Holy Spirit according to His will and counsel, our motives will be pure.

Proverbs 16:9 – "A man's heart plans his way, but the Lord determines his steps".

God prepared in advance the steps you are to take and directs you in them. That is why it so important to seek Him when making decisions.

Proverbs 16:18 – "Pride comes before destruction, and an arrogant spirit before a fall".

An arrogant spirit is one that puts one's own needs and desires before others.

Proverbs 16:25 – "There is a way that seems right to a man, but its end is the way to death".

This could mean spiritual, physical or emotional death – separation from God, death of the project or death of relationships.

Proverbs 16:28 – "A contrary man spreads conflict, and a gossip separates close friends". Contrary - that is a word we don't want to be known by. It means *"perverse, deceitful tongue, foolish."* This attitude of the heart causes trouble for everyone else by gossiping (which is slander) for the purpose of promoting one's own agenda. Gossip can destroy relationships quicker than you can sneeze. If you have ever been on the receiving end of being slandered, you know what I mean. It is harmful, hurtful and will always get back to the one you are talking about. Close friends are separated by gossip.

These verses are a lot to take in, but these are words for life regarding your plans and direction. The word *plan* from the above verses, gives the meaning of: *to calculate, devise, invent, think about, consider.* The word *directs* means *to be firmly established and directed aright, to send toward, established, prepared, restored.* If you study the verses with these definitions in mind, you will see how to apply them to your life for following the Lord's direction in planning for what is around the bend in the road. The plan should always include trusting God.

During Old Testament days, God led people in different ways. In the book of Exodus, a cloud led them by day and a pillar of fire by night. Or, God spoke directly to them, as He did to Abraham.

But the Spirit of God given through Jesus led New Testament believers, just as He leads believers today. Read what the prophet Isaiah said about Jesus.

> The Spirit of the LORD will rest on him, a Spirit of wisdom and understanding, a Spirit of counsel and strength, a Spirit of knowledge and of the fear of the LORD.
> Isaiah 11:2 HCSB

The Messiah, Jesus, is more richly endowed with a three-fold fullness of the Spirit:

1. *Wisdom and understanding* for leadership.
2. *Counsel and might* to carry out God's wise plans.
3. *Knowledge and the fear of the Lord* for holiness.

The fulfillment of this Word is found in Matthew 3:16–17 when the Spirit of God descended like a dove to rest on Jesus. Then God identified Jesus as His Beloved Son. Therefore, since we have received the Holy Spirit upon salvation, let us live by the Spirit and walk by the Spirit of Christ Jesus. Galatians 5:25 (NKJV) says, "If we live by the Spirit, let us also walk in the Spirit".

To walk in the spirit implies both direction and empowerment. Making decisions and choices according to the Holy Spirit's guidance and acting upon it with the spiritual power He supplies means falling in line behind the leader. The leader is God Himself through Jesus by the Holy Spirit, all working together to give you direction for life.

To be led by the Spirit is to have an active, personal involvement with the Lord Jesus. It indicates an on-going activity in the life of the believer.

A couple of years ago, my husband and I moved from the city where we had lived for over forty years. This move meant saying goodbye to lifelong friends, our church home of thirty–eight years and everything near and dear to us. It meant saying goodbye to teaching Bible Study that I had done for years.

When we moved in the summer, I had already committed to teach before I knew we were moving. So my sweet husband told me that if I wanted to keep that commitment for the fall, he would drive me the five hours each week so I could complete my commitment. And that is what he did.

It happened that I was teaching from the book of 2 Timothy. This book of the Bible is the last letter the Apostle Paul wrote and the last word Timothy heard from him. So, it was very emotional for me because it was my goodbye to a class of women I had taught for so long.

For some reason in the fall semester, I used a different Bible than I normally used. This one was new and I was not as familiar with how the books and chapters flowed on the pages. Then, in the last week of my study, as I read the last few verses of 2 Timothy, I turned the page for more.

The page was blank.

As I looked at that blank page, I was overwhelmed with grief and thought, *this is what my life looks like right now. Blank. I don't know what is ahead for me.*

No sooner had I thought these things than I sensed God in my spirit saying, *what looks blank to you, I have already filled. I know exactly what your future holds – trust me.*

Rock Solid Trust

Trust means to be confident and secure in something or someone, and as I thought about it, I remembered one of my favorite passages of scripture:

> Trust in the Lord with all your heart and lean not on your own understanding; in all your ways acknowledge him and he will make your paths straight.
> Proverbs 3:5–6

> *"Trust means to be confident and secure in something or someone."*

In that moment, I had immediate peace because I knew I could be confident in Him with my security. I began to pray, *Lord, I do trust you with my life and my future and I thank you in advance for it. Because my understanding is flawed by my human nature and grief, all I see is a blank page, but you know what is written on it and I am confident you have gone before me and paved a path for me.*

One month later, as I sat in my remote home, I received an unexpected invitation to speak and teach through a radio program. I was shocked! But as I prayed about accepting and spoke with a spiritual mentor, I remembered God's promise. The page that looked blank to me, God had already filled.

So I am thankful. I am thankful for God who goes before me preparing the way in which I am to go. He provided a way for me to continue teaching for a season, even from a remote location.

If He will do something new in my life, He can surely do something new in your life. Trust Him with your present and with your future. He will make a way for you. "Behold, I will do a new thing; now it shall spring forth; shall you not know it? I will even make a way in the wilderness, and rivers in the desert" (Isaiah 43:19 KJV).

Father, what a blessing it is to know you, to trust you and feel secure in your loving arms. I pray for our readers and beyond, that you will teach us to love one another and that you will teach us to trust you with the blank pages of our lives. Thank you for guiding our footsteps to the places you have gone before in order to make a way for us. Amen

Trust Building Action

And so what can we learn from all of this? We learn that our plans fail without godly counsel and seeking direction from God. The plans may seem right to you, but God will know the intentions of your heart. And that which is breathed out of your mouth will reveal your motives to others.

But God has given you a way for wisdom in making plans that will succeed. And that is to allow His Spirit to lead you in the best direction, guiding you in the decision-making process.

The result of being led by the Spirit is the fruit you will bear: Love, joy, peace, patience, kindness, goodness, faithfulness, gentleness and self-control.

You may remember playing Follow the Leader as a child. There was always a leader and everyone else followed. If the leader didn't know where he was going or where he was leading you, the end result could be disastrous. Not so with God. He will not lead you anywhere without a plan for you in that place.

He may give you direction that is the complete opposite of the plans you have made. But one thing I know: *His direction is always for our benefit and His glory.* It will always serve a purpose.

Follow Jesus. You can't go wrong with Him.

> Then Jesus spoke to them again: 'I am the light of the world. Anyone who follows me will never walk in the darkness but will have the light of life'.
> John 8:12 HCSB

Questions for Personal Growth:

- In John 8:12, what lesson is Jesus teaching?

- How can this lesson be applied to your life to build trust?

- What promise do you see for your future?

Trusting in Jesus removes the darkness of confusion, sin and spiritual death. He is the Way, Truth, Life; no one goes to the Father apart from Him. Would you trust Him today with your life for eternity? Pray in that way.

CHAPTER 7
R.E.A.D. for Optional Study

Using the READ method of study, write your observations of the verse, example, application and direction for you from the scripture below.

> The Lord had said to Abram, 'Leave your country,
> Your people and your father's household
> And go to the land I will show you'.
> Genesis 12:1

R

E

A

D

CHAPTER 8

Trust When Suffering

*Praise be to the God and Father of our Lord Jesus Christ,
the Father of compassion and the God of all comfort...*
2 Corinthians 1:3

Suffering from illness and external circumstances is not new to this generation. You have read about the suffering of Jehoshaphat and David. But in our own lives, we tend to focus on our suffering without looking beyond to learn from the suffering of others. And we certainly don't want to think there may be a lesson God has in it for us. And yet, the Bible is filled with those who suffered but were able to look beyond it to hope for deliverance and healing. How did they do this? By trusting the Lord their God. And every once in a while, we hear about someone in our generation who did the same and lived to tell the story. My friends, Kim and Doug, are an example of trusting God through extreme and unusual suffering. Here is their story in Kim's words.

> *"Mrs. Shirley, his situation is dire. You asked for brutal honesty. To quantify it, statistically he has a five percent chance to live."*

In that moment, holding my four month old daughter, I reached deep down into the roots of my faith and was reminded that 'nothing is impossible with God'. That quick, yet powerful, verse ushered me into a season of trusting the Lord in ways I had yet to experience.

That was in August of 2009. I've never written anything about this, but I'm in a season of desiring to boldly give God glory without apology.

After multi-organ complications due to sepsis, being in a drug-induced coma for almost a month, two heart attacks, the threat of amputations, eight surgeries, six weeks in ICU, time in a wound care facility, and almost a year of physical therapy, Doug recovered and slowly learned to walk again!

God performed a miracle and saved his life...in more ways than one! In fact, they named his ICU room "The Miracle Room."

Our church family here in Texas was incredible. Within an hour, the waiting room was packed! So many of you were there for us (near and far) in numerous ways for months and months - just too many to list, but you know who you are. From prayer, encouragement, medical knowledge and wisdom, communications, a place for me to stay for a month that was near the hospital, babysitting, meals and groceries, finances, driving Doug to daily therapy, and just being a listening ear, you were there. We say thank you, praise the Lord and give Him all the glory for saving Doug's life!

And in many ways, I was saved too! All that I had known of the Lord, plus all He taught me as He carried me throughout that year proved to be true. Not only did I learn to trust The Great I AM even more during one of the deepest, darkest valleys of my life (Psalm 23), I also witnessed the power of encouragement as I set my gaze on Him in order to run the daily, sometimes moment by moment, race before me. (Hebrews 12). Looking back, I am thankful for that season in many ways, but mainly because I learned that He is the foundation of every valley – one that cannot be shaken!

What a tremendous testimony of trusting God to see them through a hard season of suffering in the life of this sweet family.

When you read about the Apostle Paul from the New Testament, his story is wrought with hardships. In 2 Corinthians 1:8–9, Paul mentions the affliction he endured while in Asia. He may have been referring to his time in Ephesus, but the time and location are not certain. The point is, he suffered. It was so severe, in fact, the hardship seemed like a death sentence. He was burdened, in despair and felt weighted down by it. And yet, he looked at his suffering as a time to practice his faith and trust in God. He said, "Indeed, in our hearts we felt the sentence of death. But this happened that we might rely not on ourselves but on God who raises the dead" (2 Corinthians 1:9).

When you suffer, are you able to see the reality of God's character and purpose in the middle of it all? It is a difficult thing to do when you are not prepared to see it from that point of view. Let's back up in 2 Corinthians 1 and read Verses 3 through 7. These verses are critical to understanding the character of God and how it applies to your life during suffering.

> Praise be to the God and Father of our Lord Jesus Christ, the Father of compassion and the God of

all comfort, who comforts us in all our troubles, so that we can comfort those in any trouble with the comfort we ourselves have received from God.
2 Corinthians 1:3-4

The theme of these verses is mercy and comfort. God is merciful. He not only gives us comfort, but He teaches us how to comfort others. When you read Kim's story, you saw a modern day example of numerous people extending comfort to her family in their time of suffering. God comforted them through others. Mercy is a spiritual gift God gives to some believers. For them, extending mercy comes easily and naturally. But for others, it is a learned behavior that comes through prayer and following the Lord's leading to extend comfort where needed. It is God's character and can become yours as you are conformed more and more into the image of Christ. The more you grow spiritually, the more prepared you are not only to extend comfort, but also to receive comfort when you suffer. Growing in the Lord is trusting in the Lord.

> *"God is merciful. He not only gives us comfort, but He teaches us how to comfort others."*

There is a promise in 2 Corinthians 1:10; "He has delivered us from such a deadly peril, and He will deliver us. On Him we have set our hope that He will continue to deliver us".

I absolutely love this verse! God delivers! Not only has He done so in the past, but also He is delivering right this very minute. When you are facing any kind of suffering and difficulty, you cannot see the band of angels all around you, but they are there delivering you in this very moment. They are sent by God to see you through as He applies mercy and comfort (Hebrews 1:14, Psalm 91:11).

The sequence of this truth looks like this:

- He *has* delivered – This took place at the time of Jesus' death on the cross, redeeming us.
- He *is* delivering – When we are at a current place of suffering.
- Trust says – He *will* deliver out of the suffering
- Hope says – We *are* confidently trusting that deliverance will continue beyond what we can see.

Paul knew these things, but he also had trust and confidence that God would *keep on* delivering! That is hope, people! We must not lose hope in the face of trials and suffering. Hope is the confident expectation of something good. Paul was confident that his expectations of God's deliverance were good. His trust was rock solid, and that is where we want to be as well.

In 2 Corinthians 1:11, Paul requested prayer so that many would give thanks for the blessing given them through the prayers of others. But there are times when our prayers are not answered in the way we expect them to be. Perhaps an illness is not healed and death occurs when many have prayed for healing. What then? Do we still trust God? I believe the answer must be yes. If not, we will fall into despair that will be ongoing not allowing our hearts to heal. Death is a mystery. Yet, for the believer, it is the confident expectation of meeting Jesus face to face. It is our hope for dwelling with Him forever.

Or perhaps suffering is from another circumstance – shattered trust in an unwanted divorce, job loss, poverty, violence, being falsely accused or _____. You fill in the blank. All of these are hard to endure. And when you are hurting so bad you can't even think straight, much less pray, that is when the prayers of others are so important. That is when the offer of physical support is so important. That is when you need someone the most and should not isolate yourself from the opportunity to receive the love

Virginia Grounds

of God through a living person. He is your comfort and extends His mercy to you in your time of need and beyond. He is your hope, not only through His word, but also through His love.

Trust Building Action

Read 2 Corinthians 4:7-12. In verses 8 and 9, you find how Paul suffered followed by a result. Write his response beside the phrases describing suffering:

- Afflicted in every way, but not

- Perplexed, but not

- Persecuted, but not

- Struck down, but not

From Paul's testimony in 2 Corinthians 1:3–11, you find three things described:

1. The suffering (Verse 8–9).

2. The three-fold promise (Verse 10).
3. The result (Verse 3–7, 10b–11).

Questions for Personal Growth:

If you have experienced a recent hardship, write your experience from each of the following questions related to the four things described in Paul's testimony.

- Can you relate to the condition?

- Do you see any reason for the suffering?

- What is the promise you can cling to in suffering?

- What result do you see that gives you hope?

Pray 2 Corinthians 2:3–4 giving praise to God for providing a way of comfort through hardship. If you are still in the middle of it, thank Him for His promise to deliver, and trust Him for it. He is the comfort and hope given to you when life is hard.

CHAPTER 8
R.E.A.D. for Optional Study

Using the READ method of study, write your observations of the verse, example, application and direction for you from the scripture below.

> Praise be to the God and Father of our Lord Jesus Christ,
> the Father of compassion and the God of all comfort
> who comforts us in all our troubles
> so that we may can comfort those in any trouble,
> with the comfort we ourselves have received from God.
> 2 Corinthians 1:3–4

R

E

A

D

CHAPTER 9

Cornerstone of Trust

> In Him (Christ) the whole building is joined together
> and rises to become a holy temple in the Lord.
> And in Him you too are being built together
> to become a dwelling in which God lives by His Spirit.
> Ephesians 2:21–22

Skydiving is something I have not thought much about as I have never had a desire to take on that challenge. But in reading an article on this subject, I discovered some similarities in tandem skydiving and trusting God.

Tandem skydiving, or tandem parachuting, refers to a type of skydiving where a student skydiver is connected to a harness attached to a tandem instructor. The instructor guides the student through the whole jump from exit through freefall, piloting the canopy, and landing.

It exposes first-time jumpers to skydiving with minimal expectations from the student. The training may consist of many of the activities performed by any skydiving student. For example, how to exit the aircraft, how to do maneuvers in freefall, and how to deploy the main canopy themselves. However, (and this is important) the tandem master remains responsible for safe and timely parachute deployment.

Virginia Grounds

About the only thing required of the student is that he trust the tandem master enough to keep his hands off the equipment and enjoy the ride.

In previous chapters, you have read how to have faith and trust in God that is rock solid by identifying God as *The* Rock, *My* Rock and *Our* Rock. In this chapter, you will see Him as *YOUR* rock.

This chapter will take you into the pages of the New Testament to discover the rock of the Christian faith, the very one who makes our relationship with God the Father possible. That is the Lord Jesus Christ who is the rock of your salvation – the cornerstone of our faith.

In your Bible, read Ephesians 2:13–22.

Jesus Christ is the chief cornerstone upon which the Christian faith is established and built upon. What is a cornerstone? In architectural terms, it is 'the stone at the corner of two walls that unites them; specifically, the stone built into one corner of the foundation of an edifice as the actual or nominal starting point of a building.'[18]

What the verses in Ephesians 2 are talking about is that Jesus is the first of the Christian faith. The apostles and prophets were the first to serve the Christian faith through their preaching and teaching, with God's Word being the foundation upon which the faith was, and is, being built.

A few years back, we lived in a neighborhood that was not completed; therefore, construction was ongoing. Each day you could see houses being built. It seemed to take a while for them to get started, but once the foundation was laid, the walls went up quickly. However, nothing could be done in completing the building until the foundation had been laid first.

And so it is with the Christian faith. Without Jesus as the cornerstone of your faith, and without the foundation laid through the witness and teaching of Jesus from the prophets and apostles, there would be no Christian faith.

However, just as the builder has a plan from the architect, the master architect God put a plan in place for us through the cornerstone and foundation of the Christian faith. The plan for us to have access to God is through Jesus. When we accept Him as Lord and Savior, our body then becomes a temple of the Holy Spirit. Then, as a believer in Christ, we become a stone (a small pebble actually) that is joined together with other believers as the church built upon the cornerstone of Christ.

As the tandem skydiver jumps out of the plane, he no longer has control of his life. He has to trust the one riding behind him that he cannot see. So it is with our faith. We cannot see Jesus, but we can know and believe that He is with us to see us safely through life. When our life is in the hands of another, we cannot do anything other than trust what we cannot see. In order to live without stark-raving fear, that trust needs to be rock solid. In fact, Jesus tells us "blessed are those who have not seen and yet have believed" (John 20:29b).

> *"Blessed are those who have not seen and yet have believed."*
> *John 20:29b*

Back in the Old Testament again, God gave us a picture of Jesus coming from Him, the Rock, in Exodus 17:1-7. In these verses, you find a sequence of events.

- The people complained
- Moses cried out to God
- God answered, instructed, promised
- But Moses, in anger, did it his way
- Yet, God still provided life-giving water for the people.

For some reason, I had the image in my mind of a stream trickling out of the rock, but that is not the case. There were thousands of thirsty people there and a stream would not have been enough. The Bible tells us in Isaiah 48:2, "They did not thirst when he led them through the deserts; he made water flow for them from the rock; he split the rock and water *gushed* out". [Emphasis added]

God provided abundant, overflowing life-giving water for thirsty souls.

Now, let's turn back to the New Testament to see how this rock is described. "For they drank from the spiritual rock that accompanied them, and that rock was Christ" (1 Corinthians 10:1-4).

The rock, from which the water came, and the manna spoken of, are viewed by the writer Paul as symbolic of the spiritual sustenance God's people experienced in the desert through Christ, the bread of life and the living water.

That rock was Christ – everything you have read throughout this book has been for the purpose of bringing us to this point. God *the* Rock, God *my* Rock, God *our* Rock is *your* Rock Jesus Christ, the Chief Cornerstone.

John 10:30 tells us that Jesus and the Father are one; therefore, just as God was in the desert so was Jesus. The rock in the desert gushing water to sustain life is representative of the Living Water we have today to sustain our lives. That is Jesus Himself living in us by His Spirit for those who trust and believe in Him.

> "God *the* Rock, God *my* Rock, God *our* Rock is *your* Rock Jesus Christ, the Chief Cornerstone."

Jesus said, "If anyone is thirsty, let him come to me and drink. Whoever believes in me, as the Scripture has said, streams of living water will flow from within him" (John 7:37-38).

This Living Water is for anyone who will come to Him. No matter where you are in life, no matter your past, no matter your lifestyle, appearance or financial condition; Jesus died one time for all mankind in order to provide forgiveness of sin and access to God. He came to wash clean and save the lost. He is your Rock of

Salvation, the Cornerstone of your faith and the Living Water to fill your thirsty soul with the only water that will satisfy – the water from the Rock that is Jesus.

Our lives are under construction as we are being prepared and fitted for our final destination. The church is under construction and we as living stones are just a small part of it. The stones will not cease to be added until the end of time because God desires that none should perish but that all would have eternal life.

As a building is constructed, its strength to stand comes from each part of the construction, each brick, each stone built upon another working together to keep the building strong. This reference to believers as stones is to encourage the unity of all to keep God's church strong. The key is in believers joining together in harmony for His purpose. What is His purpose for what you are constructing? Is it being built upon a strong foundation? Is the cornerstone lined up correctly? These are questions I believe we should all ask regarding anything we are part of directing or in which we participate. The answer should always be to look to the Master Architect for answers, which is God Himself.

In review, we have traced God in the lives of people from the Old Testament to the New when God came to earth in the form of man – Jesus.

Moses, David and Jehoshaphat all had songs of praise. What I want you to see today is that Jesus, the Rock of your Salvation – He is your song of praise.

- Like Moses, you can trust Him when others do not and praise Him for His provision.
- Like David, you can trust Him when exhausted and praise Him for His strength.
- Like Jehoshaphat, you can trust Him when threatened, and praise Him for His deliverance in fighting your battles.
- Like Paul, you can trust him in your suffering knowing He is the God of all comfort and mercy.

What does your song of praise say? What have you trusted Him to do in your life? It all begins with believing in Jesus and calling upon His name to be saved. His forgiveness of sin and gift of eternal life are certainly enough to sing a song of praise about.

Just as you saw the difference in The Rock and a rock, you find that difference between Jesus the Cornerstone and Peter. As Peter used the term 'rock' figuratively of Jesus in I Peter 2:7, perhaps it was because he could relate to the name. Read John 1:40–42. Simon was the brother of Andrew who was one of the first to follow Jesus. When Andrew took Simon to Jesus, Jesus took one look at him and said, "You are Simon, son of John. You will be called 'Cephas'" (which means rock).

Now read Matthew 16:18. Again, Jesus is speaking. "And I tell you that you are Peter, and on this rock I will build my church, and the gates of Hades will not overcome it". This is Simon Peter (Cephas) – rock. The name Peter means rock, but that is where the comparison stops. There are two Greek words for rock in these verses.

1. *Petra is a mass of rock, a type of sure foundation. It is solid and immovable.*
2. *Petros is a small stone or boulder that is easily moved or tossed.*

In Verses 4 and 6 of 1 Peter 2, the Greek word *Petra* is used in reference to Jesus. He is the Living Stone and the Chief Cornerstone, solid and immovable, a sure foundation. He is the way your trust can be rock solid!

But in Verse 5, believers are also referred to as living stones but with the Greek word *Petros*. Peter's name comes from that same Greek word. He is a small stone that is easily moved. The same applies to believers today. Can you relate to Peter's name? Are you easily moved or swayed by the opinions of others? There was a time in Peter's life when he denied Christ after swearing he would die for Him. Is your foundation strong enough to keep your faith standing even in the face of adversity? It can be strong by trusting in the Rock, Petra, who is Jesus.

Jesus is not only the first stone laid on the foundation of your faith, but He is the last placed upon completion. He is the Alpha and Omega, the Beginning and End. When you place your trust in Him, you will not be put to shame by stumbling and falling. Trusting in Him makes you strong. He is able to carry the weight of your life and burdens without crumbling under the pressure because He is solid and immovable. He was with you at the beginning and He will be with you at the end. Life *in Him* is life *with Him*. His Spirit lives in you. You are the temple built upon the Cornerstone, Jesus. He has determined the construction and design for your life. How awesome is that!

And then, just as he changed Peter's name, one day He will give us a white rock with our new name on it. (Revelation 2:17) What will your new name be? How will Jesus see you? We don't know the answer to that. What we do know is that we as believers are being used as living stones for the building of the church upon the Cornerstone of Jesus. He lines up our faith. He is our guide through the final construction.

Trust Building Action

I pray that you will stand upon the solid Rock which is Christ Jesus and place your faith and trust in Him for all things in your life. Strengthen your trust and faith by a daily study of the Bible using a study method such as the READ method described in the beginning of this book. In so doing, you are not just reading, but understanding and applying God's Word to your life. Pray daily, believing and trusting Him. Reading the truth of God's Word, seeing the examples given, applying the lesson to your life and asking God for direction.

Questions for Personal Growth:

- Can you identify with the tandem skydiving story as it relates to your faith? How?

- A Thought to ponder. Where is salvation found?

> Salvation is found in no one else, for there is no other name under heaven given to men by which we must be saved.
> Acts 4:12

And on that, dear friends, you can trust.
Write your song of praise using the songs of Moses and David as examples.

CHAPTER 9
R.E.A.D. for Optional Study

Using the READ method of study, write your observations of the verse, example, application and direction for you from the scripture below.

> ... God's people and members of God's household,
> built on the foundation of the apostles and prophets,
> with Christ Jesus himself as the chief cornerstone.
> Ephesians 2:19c–20

R

E

A

D

CHAPTER 10

Trusting the Process Patiently

> But we ought always to thank God for
> you, brothers loved by the Lord,
> because from the beginning God chose you to be saved
> through the sanctifying work of the Spirit
> and through belief in the truth.
> 2 Thessalonians 2:13

My sweet friend, Laura Howell, posted something on Facebook that caught my attention. In her words,

> "I have this balsamic reduction sauce I make that well, I unashamedly want to drink the stuff. Buttery, sweet, delicious. But I rarely make it because I don't like the process. I'm an impatient cook and dislike having to wait for one thing to happen before I can do the next. When cooking, I'm all about instant gratification. Smells good, I want to eat it now. But the process is what makes it so good.
>
> I mean, I love licking the cake batter spoon, but I don't want a slice (or a glob) of batter. No, I want a slice of chocolate cake with cream cheese frosting. So I have to

let that delicious batter sit in the oven for 25 minutes, and I have to let it cool, and I have to mix up the frosting and let it set. I have to trust the process to get the end result I want.

The Lord is "cooking up" incredible things with your obedience and faithfulness. But you have to trust Him. You have to trust His process. The result will be something that's far better than you can imagine because as the Psalmist said, "Oh, taste and see that the Lord is good! Blessed is the man who takes refuge in him! Oh, fear the Lord, you his saints, for those who fear him have no lack!" (Psalms 34:8-9, ESV)

What is one of the most difficult things about trusting the Lord? Could it be that we are trusting Him for something we want right now? Yes, I believe that one of the most difficult things about trusting the Lord is the waiting. Believe it or not, impatience is not a virtue. It is in the waiting that God works to accomplish His purpose – to teach us about something that may be lacking in our lives. However, impatience wants to rob us of the benefit that waiting can provide. In her Bible Study workbook titled *Discerning the Voice of God*, Priscilla Shirer describes impatience as a thief. What an interesting thought, but so true. A thief robs us of something important to us – in this case patience.

"Impatience is a thief that robs us of the best path because we are not willing to wait for it to be revealed." – Priscilla Shirer.[19]

When an athlete puts himself in the position to run, he has to wait for the starting signal. If he rushes the

> "Impatience is a thief that robs us of the best path because we are not willing to wait for it to be revealed." – Priscilla Shirer

start, He will either have to start over, or be disqualified. In the same way, if we rush ahead of God and what He has prepared for us we never know what we will miss along the way. God uses the waiting process to complete the work He has begun in us.

Because we have trusted Jesus as Savior, we may tend to think that life will be without difficulty. This is simply not true because we live in a fallen world. There will be trials and tribulations. There will be natural disasters. When a storm came while the disciples were in a boat with Jesus, they became very frightened. Jesus said to them; "'You of little faith, why are you so afraid?' Then he got up and rebuked the winds and the waves, and it was completely calm" (Matthew 8:26).

God uses the ups and downs of life to grow our faith in Him. Accepting His salvation is the beginning of an eternal relationship with God. Our earthly journey is in preparation for what lies ahead, and salvation is the beginning of a process called sanctification. Sanctification is the ongoing work of the Holy Spirit to grow us in our faith in such a way that our trust is rock solid. Sanctification means to be set apart for the Lord, to be consecrated for holiness. As God works this process in us, our faith is strengthened. As our faith is strengthened, we are better equipped to be strong and fearless through the difficulties in life.

According to 1 Thessalonians 3:13, the purpose of sanctification is to purify our hearts so that we will be blameless before God when Jesus comes with all His saints to claim His church. Therefore, waiting patiently for the Lord to work in our lives is something that has a far-reaching goal. However, we in our human minds can't always understand that the waiting is for a far greater purpose. Waiting upon God requires trust on our part. It requires wisdom and knowledge of who He is, where He is and His purpose to prepare us for our eternity with Him.

For the holy character we need, we have to understand that sanctification is not vicarious. It cannot be transferred from one person to another like a bank draft. It is individual. It is a possession that is built up little by little as we grow and act in obedience to the Word of God.

In fact, the Bible says that you were *chosen* for sanctification: "...from the beginning God has chosen you for salvation through sanctification by the Spirit and through belief in the truth" (2 Thessalonians 2:13, NKJV). It is the predetermined state for believers set by God. He calls us by His grace, and we are to pursue that which He has called us to – the Christian journey of faith, trusting God when we want to rush ahead. It is a process developed over time as we allow ourselves to be set apart for God by our faith and trust in the Lord Jesus Christ. By the power of the Holy Spirit, God works in our hearts to bring about change for holiness. We are to simply trust the process.

Patiently Trusting

Laura's story is such a good example of what happens when we trust the process with God. He is at work within us to bring about a good result. Part of the process of trust is patience. But when we feel God is leading us to do something and it doesn't happen right away, our human nature urges us to rush ahead. However, God is working for our good. His timing is not our timing. He is working, and we are to be patient.

There are so many lessons to learn about patience from the Word of God. First, patience is a fruit of the Spirit. The Spirit of Christ lives within us. Since patience is His fruit, we have the power within us to endure trials as we wait for Him to work His process in whatever situations we encounter. We are to, not only live by the Spirit, but follow the leading of the Holy Spirit for being patient.

The actions and attitudes of one who is being sanctified, are described in scripture:

> Therefore, as God's chosen people, holy and dearly loved, clothe yourselves with compassion,

> kindness, humility, gentleness and patience. Bear with each other and forgive whatever grievances you may have against one another. Forgive as the Lord forgave you. And over all these virtues put on love, which binds them all together in perfect unity.
> Colossians 3:12-15
>
> Be kind and compassionate to one another, forgiving each other, just as in Christ God forgave you.
> Ephesians 4:32, NIV

There is a lot to take in from these verses. First, what do you learn about God? He has chosen you to be holy and loved by Him. You see also that He has forgiven you. You find that He gives you peace through Christ the Messiah, and that He has called us *all* to be one body in Christ – that is the church.

Next, you are able to clearly see that being chosen carries responsibility. Think back again from your school days to the relay games played where teams were chosen and divided. When you were chosen for a team, you couldn't just stand there and do nothing. You had responsibility to the team to do your part. You had to run the race.

And so it is with God. He has chosen us to run the race of faith requiring responsibility. That responsibility is to *put on heartfelt compassion, kindness, humility, gentleness, patience, acceptance, and forgiveness. And let the peace of God control your hearts.*

This list in Colossians represents virtues of Jesus. These virtues of Jesus are developed in us as we are conformed to the image of Christ (Romans 12:2). To be conformed means to be made like the form of another person or thing. When we give up our old way of thinking and acting and take on the virtues of Christ, we are, therefore, being conformed to His image. When we do, we are transformed – changed from the inside out by the Holy Spirit.

However, this transformation does not take place all at once. The process of sanctification takes time. And so, be patient as God does His work of sanctification in your life.

We have to take the responsibility of living a Christian life seriously. God has chosen us and forgiven us. He has made us a new creation in Christ. But old habits are hard to break. Are we willing to let go of old habits and patterns in order to allow our lives to be transformed?

Salvation began with God's love for us. A love that is unconditional, no strings attached. That love is given by the grace of God as His free gift. It is the perfect bond of unity – the glue that binds us together as one body in Christ.

If you take two pieces of paper and put them together without glue, they will separate when dropped. The same is true with people. If you put people together in a group to accomplish a task, but there is no love demonstrated by word or deed, the group will separate without accomplishing what they were meant to do. Unity in the body of Christ comes when we are kind to one another, compassionate, forgiving – and most of all, when we allow the love of Jesus to flow through us. Then we can accomplish the work set before us for the common cause of Christ.

God has given us freedom of choice. So to be compassionate, kind, loving, forgiving and patient is a choice. That is what the scripture means when it says to *put on* these things. We have the power of decision-making to say *yes, I will show compassion*; or *no, I will not*.

That is how sanctification works in us. It is a process of transforming our lives as the chosen of God to be more like Jesus every day. So, back to our original point. Patience. Patience is a virtue of Jesus. It is certainly not an easy one for us without the peace of Jesus controlling our hearts. Sometimes we rush ahead of God and second-guess His plans for us, causing us tremendous problems. However, when we exercise patience and seek the wisdom of God, the peace of Jesus pervades our lives.

Trust Building Action

The Biblical definition of patience is *endurance, perseverance, steadfastness, forbearance, slowness in avenging wrongs*. Patience is also *abiding under* meaning to live under the leadership of Christ.

We are to be patient when circumstances are pressing us down. We are to wait to avenge wrongs so as not to attack out of anger. We are to persevere – to move forward by faith, even when we don't understand, and trust God for the outcome.

Questions for Personal Growth:

- Read Hebrews 12:2. What can you learn about patience from this verse?

- What was Jesus looking to as He endured the cross?

- Read Hebrews 12:1. What are you to set aside as you run the race of life?

- Who do you look to as you run?

I love what Hebrews 12:2 tells us about patience. We are to run this race of faith with endurance – being patient in the process of being conformed more and more into the image of Christ. The Holy Spirit of God will continue to work within us through eternity. We cannot expect perfection until then because this journey of faith is a process of choosing to trust God and to live accordingly. You might say the oven baking us won't be turned off until we are done. He will continue to work in us until we meet Him face to face.

But in the meantime, you can be encouraged knowing God has chosen you, dear friend, to be His very own. Therefore, let us run with endurance the race that lies before us, keeping our eyes on Jesus, the author and perfecter of our faith. He knew the joy to come as He endured the cross, and therefore, pressed on to complete His purpose on earth. Jesus finished His assignment – He endured the cross taking our sin upon His sinless body; He finished *well* and perfectly!

We can trust God's process to get us to the end result He desires.

Heavenly Father, none of us like the difficulties of life. We all want things to be easy and smooth sailing all the time. But we recognize that is not reality. This world does have troubles, more all the time. But because of your spirit within us, we have the strength to endure when trials come our way. We have the power to press on as we wait for you. We have the love of Jesus to teach us how to love without strings attached. And so we thank you for choosing us, for loving us, for working in us day by day to conform us more and more into the image of Christ for your glory. Amen

CHAPTER 10
R.E.A.D. for Optional Study

Using the READ method of study, write your observations of the verse, example, application and direction for you from the scripture below.

> May he strengthen your hearts
> so that you will be blameless and holy
> in the presence of our God and Father when
> our Lord Jesus comes with all his holy ones.
> 1 Thessalonians 3:13

R

E

A

D

CHAPTER 11

Tools for Rock Solid Trust

Praise be to the God and Father of our Lord Jesus Christ,
who has blessed us in the heavenly realms
with every spiritual blessing in Christ.
Ephesians 1:3

When Paul wrote the letter to the saints in Ephesus, he began by reminding them of what they had in Jesus and God the Father. These same benefits belong to believers today. They are applied to our lives, but we tend to forget or become complacent at times. And so, in order to build our trust, we can use reminders as tools of hope to build strong faith and trust.

Just as building crews make use of their tools for construction, and were gifted in different areas of expertise, so we as believers have tools and talents.

Every believer in Jesus has been gifted in a way unique to them. (Romans 12:6) Each one is to employ their gift(s) for the building up of the body of Christ – the Church. Our trust is strengthened as we pick up the tools of our faith and press on toward the finish.

Some of the tools of faith are found in Ephesians 1:3-11. Read these verses and fill in the blanks to follow.

According to Verse 3, what has God the Father done for you in the heavenly realms?

Tool #1 - *Recognize* that you are _____.

Every spiritual blessing and all of the good things that follow in this passage are in Christ Jesus. He is how we are blessed. It is the presence of the Holy Spirit in our lives that guarantees the future heavenly blessings in Jesus.

Tool #2 – *Be thankful* that you have been _____ (Verse 5).

Adoption is a process. It is *the act or process of giving official acceptance or approval to something.*[20] In the New Testament Greek, it means *the nature and condition of the true Disciples of Christ, who by receiving the Spirit of God into their souls become the sons of God.*

Adoption is costly. Couples pursuing adoption for a child must pay a high price for the process. God paid a high price for us to become His children. Sin separated mankind from God for generations until being put into the position of becoming God's children through redemption – a high price paid through the sacrifice of God's only begotten Son - Jesus. Because He bought us back for Himself, adoption becomes our nature and condition as we place our trust in Jesus. God has chosen us to be His very own.

Adopted children are chosen. How were you chosen? (Verse 4).

Tool #3 – *Accept and Acknowledge* His _____.

The Bible tells us it is by grace that we have been saved and that not of ourselves, but by the free gift of God in Christ Jesus (Ephesians 2:8). Therefore, when we accept this free gift of grace, we are acknowledging His love and Jesus sacrifice for us. By accepting His grace, we place our trust in Him.

According to Verse 7, how does His grace impact our lives?

Tool #4 – *Be Confident*, you have been _____.

Rock Solid Trust

Redemption means rescuing someone from captivity. It means paying a price to get back what you already possess. In Jesus, we have been redeemed. His blood on the cross was the price paid for you and me to get back to right standing with God. It restores our relationship with God that was broken with Adam and Eve.

What is the second promise you have from Verse 7?

Tool #5 – *Live Pure*, you have been _____.

With redemption comes forgiveness. Once you are forgiven, God says He will remember your sin no more. How wonderful it would be if we could extend the same forgetfulness to the sins of others when we say we forgive them.

From Verse 8, how was His grace applied?

Tool #6 – *Experience His grace* that has been _____ on you.

Lavished is such a rich sounding word, isn't it? It sounds like the most expensive, thick and rich lotion you have ever generously applied all over your body. That is God's grace. The most expensive and lavish ointment God has to give, and He gives it to us freely. It is for you – for your sins and mine – that we can live with Him forever. God's grace to cover our sins – lavished on us generously. That's how much God loves us that He would give His Only Begotten Son to die in our place so we can live forever. How can we not trust a love like that? Experience it with a heart open to receive His grace.

> "God's grace. The most expensive and lavish ointment God has to give, and He gives it to us freely."

Read Ephesians 1:13–14. Having been included in Christ when

Virginia Grounds

you heard the Word of truth, the gospel of your salvation and you *believed in Him*, what took place in your life according to these verses?

Tool #7 – *You have been sealed*. Therefore, *Trust* the 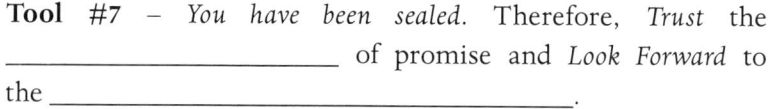 of promise and *Look Forward* to the _____.

When you place your trust in Christ Jesus, believing in Him, the Holy Spirit immediately comes into your life. He seals you for eternity with Jesus.

Trust Building Action

You have been given seven tools from Ephesians 1 as trust building reminders of who you are in Christ and how much God loves you. Use these tools when your trust is weakened, shattered or anytime you have doubt.

If you have any doubts about going to Heaven, think back and ask yourself these questions: Have I ever believed and accepted the love of God through Jesus? Have I understood that His grace covers my sin? Do I understand the meaning of redemption and what it means for me? Have I accepted the forgiveness of God and have I forgiven myself? Do I accept the blessings of God as my inheritance for eternity? Most important – do I believe Jesus for all these things? Have I asked Him to be my Savior?

The Bible tells us that those call upon the name of Jesus will be saved. Be assured that if you have done so, you will be in Heaven with Him one day.

Close your lesson in a prayer of praise for all these benefits you have out of God's grace. Your prayer of praise is the most effective tool you have for building a trust that will carry you through whatever circumstances you experience.

Trust is a day by day experience. And for those who have been deeply wounded, it takes time for trust to be built. But understanding that God loves you and is with you through the pain is critical for healing. The Lord's desire is that you trust Him one day at a time, one moment at a time as He keeps you close to Him and equips you to grow in grace and victory. The sum of it all is this: "LORD Almighty, blessed is the one who trusts in you." (Psalm 84:12)

Questions for Personal Growth:

- Do you know how God has gifted you?

- Which of the seven tools is most meaningful to you?

- What changes, if any, do you need to make in order to practice the seven tools and use the spiritual gift(s) God has given you?

From the acrostic *TRUST*, claim the following statements as you go forward by faith trusting in the Lord and His love for you.

Truth – Jesus loves you!

Redemption – Jesus paid the price for your sin.

Unity – Jesus breaks down barriers and unites relationships.

Sanctification – Jesus transforms lives!

Testimony – Jesus is the Word of your testimony.

CHAPTER 11

R.E.A.D. for Optional Study

Using the READ method of study, write your observations of the verse, example, application and direction for you from the scripture below.

> Praise be to the God and Father
> of our Lord Jesus Christ,
> who has blessed us in the heavenly realms
> with every spiritual blessing in Christ.
> Ephesians 1:3

R

E

A

D

CHAPTER 12

Desired Result

But those who hope in the LORD will renew their strength.
They will soar on wings like eagles; they
will run and not grow weary,
they will walk and not be faint.
Isaiah 40:31

Mercy surrounds the one who trusts in the Lord. When you grieve, suffer, are betrayed or threatened; you are surrounded by God's mercies. They are new every morning. The key to experiencing the hope and comfort that only God can give is trust.

Trust is built on faith, wisdom and knowledge. You must first believe by faith that Jesus is the Son of God who died on the cross for your sin, was buried and raised on the third day in order to redeem you for eternal life. The Bible tells us that we are blessed when we believe even though we cannot see.

Then wisdom from God is given by His Spirit. Knowledge is gained as you study the Bible for the purpose of growing your faith and your relationship with God. The greater your faith, the stronger your relationship and the deeper your trust.

Before a couple marries, something happens first. They meet, date and get to know one another before moving forward to marriage. They spend time together to grow in their relationship.

Virginia Grounds

What began as knowing *of* the person became knowing *the* person. It is in the knowing that growing occurs. It is in the growing that trust builds.

So it is with God. If you want a rock solid trust in God you have to spend time with The Rock who is God himself. You do that through prayer, Bible study, church attendance and worship.

Trust is a conscience decision. It is a discipline to practice. It is not something you see, but rather a choice you make. And finally, if you want to fully trust God, you will need to lift up the sword of the Spirit which is the Word of God. We see it as a book called the Bible, but God sees it as living, active and sharper than a two-edged sword. In John 1, the Bible says that "the word became flesh and dwelt among men." That reference is to Jesus. He is the word of God sent to live on earth to draw all men to Himself. He is the revelation of God – the message to all for salvation. He was at one time visible on earth, but now in Heaven. Therefore, we believe what we can no longer see, yet know Jesus is real – He is alive by His Spirit in those who believe.

> "Trust is a conscience decision. It is a discipline to practice. It is not something you see, but rather a choice you make."

If you look up references for trust in the Bible, you will find more than 100 verses. Use a Bible Concordance to look up some of these verses. Find one that speaks to you in a very personal way; one that will help you make the commitment to trust God more. Write it down and carry it with you as a reminder of Christ the solid rock upon which we stand. Pray it, memorize it until you begin to sense a change in your heart and mind.

One of my favorites is Psalm 56:3 "When I am afraid, I put my trust in you." It is short and easy to memorize.

Here are a few others to get you started.

- Proverbs 3:5
- Isaiah 12:2
- Isaiah 25:9
- John 14:1

Trust Building Action

Your activity for strengthening your trust in God is to read Colossians 1:13-23. Make a list of everything you see that Jesus has done for you. Pray a prayer of thanksgiving and praise to God for the work of Christ on your behalf. He is all in all!

Questions for Personal Growth:

- Write your verse(s) on trust below. Why is it so meaningful to you?

My Rock, My Hope

In desperation and despair we strive
To rely on choices of our own
But with faith in Christ the solid Rock
We are able to walk our path, never alone.

So stop your worry and let go of despair
A lifeline for you is waiting
Grab hold of trust in the solid Rock
No more fear or critical debating.

Make the choice to lean on Jesus
Trusting what you cannot see
Let go of fear, despair and selfish desire
Go forward when Jesus says *"follow Me"*.

For in Him your life is secure
The future is in His hands
So trust the Living Savior
With all your hopes and plans.

In Him is life eternal
In Him are rewards and joy
He is God's grace lavished on you
For salvation and purpose to employ.

–Virginia –

CHAPTER 12
R.E.A.D. for Optional Study

Using the READ method of study, write your observations of the verse, example, application and direction for you from the scripture below.

> But I trust in your unfailing love;
> My heart rejoices in your salvation.
> I will sing to the LORD,
> For He has been good to me.
> Psalm 13:5-6

R

E

A

D

CHAPTER 13

My Trust Building Journey of Faith

> When He comes, He will convict the world
> about sin, righteousness, and judgment.
> John 16:8 HCSB

"Virginia, what is wrong with you?" That question was asked of me by a coworker many years ago. My answer was *"I don't know what is wrong with me. I just know I am miserable."* She pointed her finger, laughed and said, *"Oh I know what is wrong with you. God has you under conviction."*

Conviction – what does that mean? I was too embarrassed to tell her I had no idea what she was talking about. But that is where my journey of faith began. I was 29 years old.

And so if you are like me and don't know the meaning of conviction, let me share with you that at the time I needed to know, there were no computers much less Google and Wikipedia. So, the old fashioned way of finding a word definition was a Webster's paper dictionary. This is the meaning I found at that time: *being convinced; strong belief. To be convicted*. Well, that was not very helpful. But with that definition, I had to ask myself the question - being convinced of what? I had to begin examining what was missing in my life. I had to question what I believed about God. Until then, all I knew of God was the rote prayer prayed before meals as a child and hunting

Easter eggs at church with my siblings. But as I searched, God led me until I found Him through my Savior Jesus Christ.

But let me back up a few years. The twenties were very difficult years for me and my young daughter. As a single Mom I struggled with all the normal things a single Mom struggles with – time, jobs, money, relationships and parenting. But in addition to those things, I struggled with grief. My own Mother died when I was 24 and my Dad when I was 27. Since I did not have faith in God to keep me grounded, I was a miserable, angry, hurting person. Relationships were destroyed by my personal pain.

Then I met and married my husband whose family were faithful believers and prayer warriors. They were different. As time went by, I began to long for what they had even though I couldn't tell you what it was. Shortly after our marriage, I began to work for a company where the leadership offered Bible Study on a weekly basis. Being raised and taught to be a 'good girl', I thought I should attend the study. Little did I know what God had in store for me! The leader gave each of us in attendance a Bible and began to teach from the book of Revelation. Revelation, really??

When my husband and I were dating, I asked what his family believed. He began to tell me some things, but what stood out to me was when he said, "They believe Jesus will come again and believers will be taken up with Him." My reaction was disbelief. "You have got to be kidding me! That is the most ridiculous statement I have ever heard." That is what I said to him.

So, how did God get my attention to lead me to Jesus? By putting me in a study of the book of Revelation and the time when Jesus will come again! I became fascinated and couldn't get enough of knowing God and His Word. One day while at the grocery story, I saw a book by Hal Lindsey titled *The Late Great Planet Earth*. I bought it and, as I read, I couldn't put it down. One night while home alone, I read the last chapter and there on the very last page was the prayer for salvation. It was like a lightbulb went off inside me and I thought, *this is* it. *This is what I have been looking for.* I got on my knees by the bed and prayed to receive Jesus. From that moment on, God gave me a hunger to know Him more and a thirst for wisdom from the Bible that is still with me today, many years later. My life was dramatically changed in that moment by my bed. God has proven Himself to me over and over again beginning with teaching me that you don't mock God or His people. He used the very thing I had mocked to draw me to Him. He ignited fire in my heart and hunger and thirst for His Word that has never been extinguished. It is still my greatest joy to study the Bible, to teach, to know Jesus and the Word of God.

And that is where my trust building journey of faith began…

Fast forward to today. If you look up the word conviction on the internet using the Webster's Merriam Dictionary, you will find a more descriptive definition than I found all those years ago. It says conviction is:

1. *The act or process of finding a person guilty of a crime especially in a court of law.*
2. *The act of convincing a person of error or of compelling the admission of a truth.*
3. *The state of being convinced of error or compelled to admit the truth.*
4. *A strong persuasion or belief. The state of being convinced.*

This would have been helpful to know years ago, but it still raises questions of what this means related to God and faith. A person would need to attend a Bible teaching church and read the Bible for themselves to begin to find the answer of what it means to 'be under conviction' from a Biblical perspective. Let me try to break it down for you.

- *The act or process of finding a person guilty of a crime especially in a court of law.* Just as justice must be served in a court of

Rock Solid Trust

law, justice must be served dividing evil from good from a spiritual perspective. God is the Righteous Judge who sent Jesus to reveal that none are righteous without Him to make them so. All have sinned and fall short of the glory of God. (Romans 3:23)

- *The act of convincing a person of error or of compelling the admission of a truth.* Sin must be identified and acknowledged in our lives. We must understand that we cannot be pure without the cleansing blood of Christ who sacrificed His life for you and me.
- *A strong persuasion or belief. The state of being convinced.* Once we admit our sinful state, ask for forgiveness and invite Jesus into our lives as our Savior, we begin our trust building journey of faith believing in Him, having been convinced of the eternal life saving grace of God; the gift freely given.

In the book of John we discover that it is Jesus who, not only saves us from our sin, but convicts us by His Spirit in a way that we are confronted and weighed down with it. "When He comes, He will convict the world about sin, righteousness, and judgment." (John 16:8 HCSB) Convicting the world about sin is in reference to an individual's unbelief and their failure to put their trust in Jesus. Only through research and Bible reading was I able to discover this truth about conviction. Only through the boldness of a believing friend was I made aware of my condition and my need.

Therefore, knowing the following verse was critical for understanding how much God loves me and pursued me. "For God so loved the world that He gave His Only Begotten Son that whosoever believes in Him shall not perish, but have everlasting life. For God did not send His Son into the world to condemn the world, but to save the world through Him" (John 3:16-17 KJV).

Knowing Jesus is a choice that only an individual can make for themselves. Billy Graham said it best, *"Our families cannot choose*

Virginia Grounds

Christ for us. Our friends cannot do it. God is a great God, but even God can't make the decision for us...we have to make our own choice.[21]"

I made that choice, but I was a young adult in my late twenties before I determined to know Jesus. I had been under conviction for eight years and didn't know it. At the age of 21, I began visiting church with a co-worker. From that moment on, there was an unsettled feeling in my soul. God called to me there, but I didn't recognize His voice. So, because of poor advice from someone close to me, I walked away and never returned to that church. The price paid, not only for me but my daughter as well, was years of misery without understanding why. Yet, God never gave up on me. He just kept wooing me to come to Him until, finally, someone got right in my face, pointed a finger and told me what I needed to hear. *God has you under conviction.* And so I searched for answers. I searched for Jesus. I knew I wanted Him as my Savior, but didn't know how to go about it. Then I read a book that explained much of what I longed to know. At the end of the book, the author wrote the prayer to pray to accept Jesus and be saved. You will find one in this book as well. It changed my life and it can do the same for you.

> "Our families cannot choose Christ for us. Our friends cannot do it. God is a great God, but even God can't make the decision for us...we have to make our own choice." – Billy Graham

God has taught me so much through the years of my faith journey, but the lessons learned from the beginning of the journey to Him still apply today.

1. *You don't mock God.* He used the very thing I had mocked to draw me to Him through studying His Book from the very last chapter. Yes, Jesus will come again!
2. *You don't walk away from God when He calls you to Himself.* He knows right where you are, and He knows your heart. I had the opportunity to come to Jesus at the age of 21 but walked away for eight miserable years. So much regret, but so great a grace and forgiveness.
3. *God Doesn't Give Up on You.* Even though He allowed me to walk away; my choice, my will, God didn't stop trying to get my attention. He never wavered in His purpose to, not only save me, but to use me for His service. And I am still serving Him today. It is still my heart's desire. Praise God for His unwavering, pursuing love.

What is your heart's desire? Do you long to know more of Jesus?

Don't be like me and turn away from the *first* opportunity to accept Jesus as Savior or to return to Him. Don't be like me and suffer for years without knowing why. Turn to Jesus now. Your life will never be the same.

That is why I am including a path for you to follow. It changed my life and it can do the same for you.

HOW DO I BECOME A CHRISTIAN?[22]

You think you're a good person. You've always tried to be the best you can be, and do what is right. The good outweighs the bad in your life. But, after all of this, do you still feel empty, unsatisfied, void and alone?

You may have even tried things such as drinking, drugs, sex, materialism, partying or hanging with a certain crowd to fill this unexplained need you have.

But, is something still missing from your life? There is One who can fill that void— God. If you've tried lots of solutions to make your life right, but none seem to work, then He is the answer.

God has given us an important manual for life—the Bible. He is the author of this book and has given significant, truthful instructions for how we can have joy, hope and peace in life. He has the answers to the problems and emptiness you may face.

You are here for a purpose, and not by accident. We were separated from God because of sin in the beginning of the world. But, God sent His Son, Jesus Christ, who lived on earth, suffered punishment, and died on a cross to pay for your sins. Three days later, He rose from the dead.

Jesus loves you, and desires to have a personal relationship with you. But, sin separates us from Him.

For all have sinned and come short of the glory of God. —ROMANS 3:23

The most important decision in your life will be whether you accept Him as your personal Lord and Savior. You must choose forgiveness and a relationship with God. This begins with repentance and turning away from your sins and old life to a new life in Christ.

The Lord is not slack concerning His promise, as some count slackness, but is longsuffering toward us, not willing that any should perish but that all should come to repentance. —2 PETER 3:9

You may think that you need to fix things or make things right in your life before you come to Christ. And many people feel that way, but it's not true!

God demonstrates His own love for us in this: While we were still sinners, Christ died for us. —ROMANS 5:8

You will be saved by the grace of God, not because you try to make things right in your life. He wants you to accept this salvation only because He loves you! It is not something to be earned ... it is a free gift.

For it is by grace you have been saved, through faith—and this not from yourselves, it is the gift of God—not by works, so that no one can boast. —EPHESIANS 2:8–9

For God so loved the world that He gave his one and only Son, that whoever believes in Him shall not perish, but have eternal life. —JOHN 3:16

Sin causes death, but because God sent His Son to die for your sins, you can have the free gift eternal life.

For the wages of sin is death, but the gift of God is eternal life in Jesus Christ our Lord.—ROMANS 6:23

All you have to do is to accept Him and confess Him as your personal Lord and Savior.

If you confess with your mouth, "Jesus is Lord," and believe in your heart that God raised Him from the dead, you will be saved. For it is with your heart that you believe and are justified, and it is with your mouth that you confess and are saved. — ROMANS 10:9–10

If you are ready to accept the gift of eternal life through Jesus, and you truly desire to ask Him into your heart to be your personal Lord and Savior, then pray this prayer:

PRAYER TO BECOME A CHRISTIAN

"Jesus, I know that I am a sinner. I believe that You died for my sins and rose from the grave so that I might have eternal life in heaven with You. I willingly repent of my sins and ask You to come into my heart and life. Take control of my words, thoughts and actions. I place all of my trust in You for my salvation. I accept You as my Lord and Savior, and this free gift of eternal life. Amen."

REFERENCES

1. Debbie Stuart, *20 Minutes a Day for the Rest of Your Life*. Available on EBay – search Debbie Stuart
2. Excerpts from the works of A. W. Tozer are used by permission of WingSpread Publishers, a division of Zur Ltd., Camp Hill, PA.
3. *The Attributes of God 1* from The A. W. Tozer Bible page 1426, KJV, Hendrickson Bibles, 2012
4. Webster's Dictionary
5. Webster's Dictionary
6. Numbers 25:1-9 NIV
7. Psalm 115:2-8
8. 2 Samuel 13:36-37, the Holy Bible
9. Genesis 1
10. Dictionary.com
11. Strong's Bible Dictionary
12. Vine's Bible Dictionary of Old and New Testament Words
13. Yahoo Web definition
14. The New Guide to Crisis & Trauma Counseling by Dr. H. Norman Wright, Regal Press 2003
15. Dr. Jack Graham, Senior Pastor, Prestonwood Baptist Church, Plano Texas
16. http://www.biblia.work/sermons/columbuschristopher/
17. Gesenius' Hebrew-Chaldee Lexicon, from www.blueletterbible.org
18. The New Unger's Bible Dictionary, Merrill F. Unger, 1988 Moody Press
19. "Discerning the Voice of God" Priscilla Shirer, Lifeway 2017
20. Merriam-Webster's Online Dictionary
21. Billy Graham, *Day by Day* (Minneapolis, MN: World Wide, 1965), December 11.
22. http://www.prestonwood.org/about/becoming-a-christian, used by permission.